*Donald McGraw Family
Children's Book
Endowment*

THE LIBRARY FOUNDATION

Serving the People of Multnomah County

Other books by Joan Dash

The World at Her Fingertips: The Story of Helen Keller
The Longitude Prize
We Shall Not Be Moved: The Women's Factory Strike of 1909

A DANGEROUS ENGINE

Benjamin Franklin,
from
Scientist
to
Diplomat

A DANGEROUS ENGINE

Joan Dash

Benjamin
Franklin,
from
Scientist
to
Diplomat

Pictures by
Dušan Petričić

Frances Foster Books

Farrar, Straus and Giroux - New York

www.fsgkidsbooks.com

Library of Congress Cataloging-in-Publication Data

Dash, Joan.
    A dangerous engine : Benjamin Franklin, from scientist to diplomat / Joan Dash ; pictures by
Dušan Petričić.— 1st ed.
        p.   cm.
    ISBN-13: 978-0-374-30669-4
    ISBN-10: 0-374-30669-9
    1. Franklin, Benjamin, 1706–1790—Juvenile literature.   2. Statesmen—United States—
Biography—Juvenile literature.   3. Scientists—United States—Biography—Juvenile literature.
4. Inventors—United States—Biography—Juvenile literature.   5. Printers—United States—
Biography—Juvenile literature.   6. United States—Foreign relations—1775–1783—Juvenile
literature.   I. Petričić, Dušan, ill.   II. Title.

E302.6.F8 D2165 2006
973.3'092—dc22
[B]
                                                                        2004063204

Dedicated to my loyal critics, Mike, Liz, Jeff, and Tony
—J.D.

I am grateful to my husband, Greg Dash,
for advice and encouragement,
for his inexhaustible willingness to listen,
and for suggesting this project to begin with.

For curious Adam and sparky Olivia
—D.P.

Contents

Part I
At Home in the Laboratory

Chapter One

The Dangling Boy

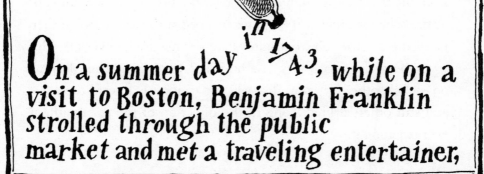

On a summer day in 1743, while on a visit to Boston, Benjamin Franklin strolled through the public market and met a traveling entertainer, a Scotsman recently arrived from Edinburgh. His name was Archibald Spencer, and he planned to earn a living by putting on science shows.

It seems he had launched this American career by means of a notice in the Boston paper announcing lecture-demonstrations for groups of twenty—but nothing like twenty ever showed up. Now Spencer was waiting for his luck to change, and in the meantime offering private lessons to individuals. Where? Right here in his booth at the market. Was Franklin interested?

Of course he was. Since childhood he had been possessed of a powerful curiosity, a need to know how things worked and why— storms, numbers, waterspouts, ant colonies, currents in the ocean. He was thirty-seven years old now and as curious as ever.

Out came a green glass tube some twenty inches long and sealed at both ends. Spencer laid it on the counter and set to work rubbing it ferociously with his hand; after a time he switched, and rubbed just as fiercely with the other hand. Shaking out a bunched-up handkerchief, he emptied its contents onto the countertop— scraps of brass foil, bits of thread, the skeletons of dried leaves. Rubbing the glass again, he held it near the little heap of oddments; at the tube's approach, the lighter bits began to twitch. Some then jumped up to the tube, but immediately threw themselves off. This was repeated several times, the brass foil leaping up, then leaping off—while other bits moved slowly and cautiously toward the glass, and still others drifted along in the direction of the glass without ever reaching it.

Either then in Boston, or later when Franklin was back home in Philadelphia, Spencer performed for him the spectacle of the Dangling Boy. The boy was small, perhaps five or six years old, and Spencer tied him up with insulating cords so that he hung horizontally, like a bird in flight. There began a vehement rubbing of the glass tube, after which Spencer laid the tube against the boy's bare foot, his other hand hovering above the child's hair. It stood on end! Rubbing the glass again, he touched the boy's nose and a spark sprang out. Then his elbow, his chin, his thumb, each time rubbing the glass as if to renew some magical power, and each time producing a fine, fat spark. It seemed the child's body was packed full of some curious substance, but what was it? Where in the body was it kept? Could others respond the same way to a rubbed glass tube?

The lecture part of Spencer's show—as he gave it in Philadelphia, where he settled for several years—was long and varied, touching on such subjects as light, gravity, the circulation of the blood, the nature of color. But there was little explanation of electricity. Apparently, Spencer didn't know much about it. In any case his career as a science showman came to an end when he transformed himself into an Anglican minister and left town for his first congregation.

Years later, when Franklin wrote his autobiography, he began the account of his scientific career with Spencer and the Boston market. Although he remembered the year as 1746, and recalled Spencer's name as Spence, his recollection was on the whole a pleasant one; the stunts, he said, were "imperfectly performed, as he

IT SEEMED THE CHILD'S BODY WAS PACKED FULL OF SOME CURIOUS SUBSTANCE.

was not very expert, but being on a subject quite new to me, they equally surprised and pleased me."

Benjamin Franklin had been born in Boston, in 1706, and most of his family remained there. It was a numerous family—seventeen children from two marriages, of whom Ben was the fifteenth child, and youngest boy. His father, Josiah, was a soap and candle maker, a churchgoing man who saw the child was bright, and thought of rais-ing him to be a minister. But education for the ministry proved to be too expensive, and after two years, at the age of ten, Ben's schooling came to an end.

Apprenticed to his father, he made soap and cut wicks for can-dles, and hated every minute of it. He dreamed of going to sea; his father, who had already lost one son to the sea, persuaded Ben to stay safe on land and apprentice himself to an older brother, James, a printer.

By that time the boy was a compulsive reader. He had always loved books, having taught himself to read at such an early age that he had no memory of not being able to. James had just returned to Boston from London, bringing a generous supply of books, maga-zines, and new ideas from the great world—that's what London was to the American colonies, the absolute center of the world, the most important place beyond the ocean. Ben devoured everything his brother brought home.

He learned printing and newspapering from James; equally im-portant, he learned from his brother to stand up to authority, the authority of his father, of the church—and, ironically, of James. When the boy was seventeen, he ran away from James and the apprenticeship, claiming his brother beat him; he traveled to New York, then Philadelphia, then all the way to London. After a year and a half he returned to the colonies and settled in Philadelphia, prepared to work hard at making a place for himself in that city as a printer and publisher.

At the time of his first meeting with Spencer, Franklin was living with his wife and children in a rented house on Market Street—a lively part of town, close to the waterfront and the courthouse, and full of shops. Franklin's shop, with his press and printing equipment, was installed on the street level, the kitchen being below in the basement, while the two floors above the shop had two narrow bedrooms apiece. But for a hardworking tradesman and his hardworking wife, the shop was the heart of the household.

It was here that Franklin printed books, pamphlets, and other people's newspapers as well as his own, the weekly *Pennsylvania Gazette*. He printed paper money, notices, and legal documents for the colony of Pennsylvania, and served as public printer for three other colonies. A corner of the shop was Philadelphia's post office, Franklin being the postmaster. He made paper, paying cash for old rags used in the process; on a small scale he was a moneylender.

Almanacs were an essential part of colonial life; people who owned no other book but the Bible could be counted on to buy an almanac every year for its store of information—tide charts, calendars, dates of fairs, lists of inns, and an abundant seasoning of proverbs and sayings. Franklin had launched *Poor Richard's Almanac* while in his midtwenties, and sold about ten thousand copies a year.

Almost six feet tall and sturdily built, he was not handsome and had little in the way of personal vanity. Recalling his early years as a printer, he said, "I dressed plain and was seen at no places of idle diversion . . . and to show that I was not above my business, I sometimes brought home the paper I purchased at the stores, through the streets on a wheelbarrow." He wanted people to see him as "an industrious, thriving young man."

His childhood had taught him that the good things of this world were in short supply and therefore had to be worked for, sometimes fought for. He learned to drive hard bargains. He fixed his eyes on the main chance and kept them there. The proverbs in *Poor Richard's Almanac* had a good deal to say about the getting and keeping of money: "Nothing but money is sweeter than honey"; "There are three faithful friends: an old wife, an old dog, and ready money"; "Light purse, heavy heart"—and he learned those lessons himself, learned them well enough that he could think about retiring within a very few years.

But Franklin had other qualities as well, enough for several personalities. Some people are the same all the way through, consistent and predictable; Franklin was "speckled." He changed, took up new roles, found new motives within himself. While he spent most of his Philadelphia years in hot pursuit of money, at the same time he devoted himself to projects that served the public and had nothing to do with money. Many began as collective efforts, dreamed of and planned by Franklin, then set in motion with the help of others. There was a fire company in Philadelphia because he brought it to life; there were also a hospital, a corps of police, an academy that later became the University of Pennsylvania, an American Philosophical Society, and a library that gave birth to America's first public library system—all due in part or whole to Franklin. He may have developed his robust sense of civic duty from the Quakers he lived among, in that Quaker stronghold of Philadelphia, the City of Brotherly Love, although he himself was never a Quaker.

However it came about, that's the way he was, a sharp dealer hungry for success yet also a resourceful do-gooder with a genius for managing projects and men. He had imagination, a lively sense of humor (low humor at times), and exceptional intelligence. When he retired, he intended to use his leisure to "read, study . . . and converse at large with such ingenious & worthy Men, as are pleased to honour me with their Friendship . . . on such Points as may produce something for the common Benefit of Mankind."

One part of the shop was the territory of his wife, Deborah, known as Debbie. Franklin had first seen her when he was a seventeen-year-old runaway, walking up Market Street after journeying from New York in a succession of small boats. Hungry, filthy, exhausted, he had spent all his money for three great rolls of bread. Eating one as he walked and carrying the other two under his arms because his pockets were stuffed with a few changes of clothing, he was conscious of looking slightly ridiculous. He heard a girl laugh. When he looked up, he saw she was laughing at him.

Now the laughing girl was his wife and business partner. She sold paper, parchment, ink, goose feathers, cheese, tea, coffee, sherry, iron stoves, spectacles, and cakes of Crown soap made by her husband's sister Jane from a secret recipe.

Debbie was apparently short-tempered and by all accounts both plain-looking and plain-spoken. Generous, warmhearted, a tender nurse at the bedside, she was also an excellent cook and a thrifty household manager, but she had no interest in books or the conversation of what her husband called "ingenious and worthy men"—except for Pappy, the one she was married to.

Their daughter, Sarah—everyone called her Sally—was born in 1743, seven years after the loss of their first child, Francis (Franky for short), who died of smallpox at the age of four. The other child was a son named William, born in 1730 or 1731—the date was uncertain, and the name of the boy's mother was unknown, except to Franklin. It was generally accepted that young Ben got some poor girl pregnant—perhaps a servant or a fishmonger in the marketplace. In his autobiography, he addressed "that hard-to-be governed passion of youth, which hurried me frequently into intrigues . . . attended with some expense and great inconvenience." He brought the infant home at the same time he married Debbie, probably choosing his wife on the condition that she would agree to raise his child. Debbie did agree, and by the time of Sally's birth, William was in his early teens, tall, good-looking, companionable, eager to do whatever his father did.

It was a small family and a small house, and they were rarely alone in it. Debbie's mother lived with them for a while. Apprentices lodged and boarded, neighbors came in and out. Nieces, nephews, and cousins once or several times removed were all made welcome, for Franklin had long since reconciled with his father and James. Alongside its ample supply of proverbs about money, *Poor Richard's Almanac* had even more about friendship.

The Market Street house was warm, not only because it was hospitable but also because of its heating system: the Pennsylvania fireplace, invented by Franklin in 1739. Nowadays called the Franklin stove, it was designed as a freestanding warming machine, arranged so that the heat would not go straight up the chimney to warm the outdoors but would instead radiate into the room. Smoke flowed through a passage in the floor, then up to the flue and outside, sparing the complexions of women in danger of being smoked alive by conventional heating.

Smoke removal proved to be a more complex problem than originally thought, and Franklin continued tinkering with the stove on and off for the next fifty years. But, when first invented, his warming machine sold well enough, especially in New England with two of Franklin's brothers, John and Peter, as salesmen. Thomas Jefferson relied on a Franklin stove later at Monticello, and there were many imitations; a London merchant made a fortune from one of the designs.

The Governor of Pennsylvania had offered Franklin a patent that would have given him exclusive rights to sales within the colony and could conceivably have been stretched to include some other colonies, in which case Franklin might have made an impressive amount of money. But he declined. "As we enjoy great advantages from the inventions of others," he said, "we should be glad of an opportunity to serve others by any invention of ours."

He took care to publish a pamphlet describing the stove and all its workings so that everyone would know whose brainchild it was. But as an inventor, and later a scientist, he was invariably fair-minded. He gave others credit when they deserved it, and he never patented anything, ever.

Now a succession of small events moved Franklin closer to early retirement. Years before, at the age of twenty-one, he had started a club, the Junto, also known as the Leather-Apron Club, its members being young workingmen with an interest in self-improvement. At first they met in taverns; later they rented quarters on Pewter Platter Alley. The Junto held serious discussions and read serious books—which led to the creation of the Library Company. Fifty people paid to join, the money was used to buy books, and any member could take one home. What's more, any "civil gentlemen" might come in to read the library's books, although only members could take them out.

There was so little publishing in the American colonies that most books had to be sent for from London, and Franklin was at times touchingly grateful for them. He wrote to the printer William Strahan, who had sent books to be sold in Franklin's shop:

> Let me have everything, good or bad, that makes a Noise and has a Run: for I have Friends here of Different Tastes to oblige with the Sight of them . . . Your authors know but little of the Fame they have on this Side the Ocean . . . Whatever [James] Thomson writes, send me a Dozen Copies of. I had read no Poetry for several years, and almost lost the Relish of it, till I met with his Seasons. That charming Poet has brought more Tears of Pleasure into my Eyes than all I ever read before. I wish it were in my Power to return him any Part of the Joy he has given me.

The Library Company depended on help from Peter Collinson, a London businessman, well-known botanist, and Quaker with affectionate ties to America. For almost fifteen years, Collinson had been acting as the library's agent, filling its members' orders for books about government, astronomy, architecture, and gardening, and such classics as *Gulliver's Travels*, *The Iliad* and *The Odyssey*, and *The Pilgrim's Progress*. In 1747 Collinson sent the usual packet of books, as requested, and with them a glass tube about two feet long; they were to rub it with a flannel pad, he said. It was probably in the same mailing that Franklin found a recent issue of a popular English publication, the *Gentleman's Magazine*, with a five-page story about research in electricity being carried out by European investigators.

He read it with lively interest. Until then Franklin had thought of electric fire as an entertainment, a parlor trick. Now he saw that experiments could be done with it. Natural philosophers (meaning scientists) were engaged in exactly such experiments, and they described their discoveries in the *Gentleman's Magazine*. In Holland, France, and Germany, perhaps at that very moment, they were carrying out their investigations, revealing invaluable truths about nature. Why shouldn't he do the same?

He had no training for it, no laboratory, no colleagues to advise him, but scientific exploration in the mid-eighteenth century was far more loosely structured than it is today—it took place in some universities and national institutes, but also in the homes of those who had the leisure for it, the interest, and some money for supplies.

Franklin turned to friends from the Library Company. Together they played with the glass tube, growing accustomed to the feel of it the way Archibald Spencer had. Rubbing the glass with flannel, they saw stray bits of material fly up to it and instantly throw themselves off. Though Franklin could never bring himself to suspend a child from the ceiling, according to the *Gentleman's Magazine* the same effects Spencer had achieved with the Dangling Boy could be produced by having an individual stand on the floor with a wax pad under his feet. The wax served as insulation that kept the electricity from dribbling away.

Franklin and his friends rubbed the glass, touched the person stationed on the wax pad, and there it was—his hair stood on end.

Sparks flew from his elbow or chin when touched with the rubbed glass. On an especially dry day the sparks were fiery.

Once people got wind of these goings-on, Franklin's house filled with curious neighbors, friends, and relatives. He placed an order with a local glassblower for more tubes. Soon everybody who wanted one could be supplied, and bit by bit a tabletop laboratory came to life in an upstairs room of the house on Market Street. The equipment was primitive, partly borrowings from Debbie's kitchen—a vinegar cruet, thimbles, a salt cellar—as well as old books with gilt bindings and old picture frames. Those who gathered in the laboratory tried the experiments described in the magazine, thought up experiments of their own, and in between invented jokes and stunts of an electrical nature. People began calling them the Franklinists.

Writing to Peter Collinson in London to thank him for the gift, Franklin said, "I never was before engaged in any study that so totally engrossed my attention and my time as this has lately done; for what with making experiments when I can be alone, and repeating them to my Friends and Acquaintance, who, from the novelty of the thing, come continually in crowds to see them, I have, during some months past, had little leisure for anything else."

There was more to the letter. Several of us, he said, "have observed some particular phenomena that we look upon to be new. I shall, therefore communicate them to you in my next, though possibly they may not be new to you, as among the numbers daily employed in those experiments on your side the water, 'tis probable some one or other has hit on the same observations." Franklin's concern, that somebody in that great world had already found whatever treasures a grubby colonial believed he was the first to dig up, would be expressed many times in the months to come.

What he couldn't know was that this project was going to alter the shape of his life, and underwrite a revolution.

Chapter Two

Elektor and Elektron

The study of electricity fell into
Franklin's lap more or less by chance,
but he could not have chosen a branch

of science better suited to someone whose schooling ended after two years. It was a young science, almost newly hatched; so little had been written about it that there was no body of learning to be digested before plunging into experiments.

In Franklin's case a lack of schooling did not mean a lack of education. He had always been a lover of books. He not only read and enjoyed whatever he could lay hands on in English but also taught himself to read Spanish, Italian, and French. He could even speak a little French, although badly. Among the books available through the Library Company were Sir Isaac Newton's *Opticks* and the works of natural philosophers—scientists—who followed where Newton led. Robert Boyle, writing at length about electricity and magnetism, was a particular favorite of Franklin's.

Boyle wrote the first book devoted entirely to electrical fire, whose history is romantic and very old. It begins with amber, which looks like stone but is really a hardened tree resin. Sought after and widely traded in the ancient world, amber was the color of gold and therefore a child of the sun, which the Greeks called *elektor*. Amber they called *elektron*. When rubbed with a cloth, a bare hand, or an animal skin, beads made of this golden stuff attracted whatever chaff or feathers or bits of thread they approached.

For the next two thousand years people argued, speculated, and developed theories to explain this attraction without learning anything more. They approached other physical puzzles the same way, by weaving theories or else consulting authorities from Aristotle to the Bible. In 1600 an English physician, William Gilbert, proposed a new way of learning about nature. Instead of inventing theories or reading Aristotle, he said, we must turn to the natural world and examine it—investigate, carry out reliable experiments. He promised that what we found would be "almost entirely new and unheard-of."

He himself had done a number of experiments on amber, using a simple instrument of his own invention, a light metal rod poised on an apex like the needle of a compass. With this rod he found other substances that attracted when rubbed, although their attractive powers were weaker than amber's; among them were diamond, amethyst, beryl, crystal, opal, and hardened sealing wax. Other substances refused to attract at all. Gilbert labeled these two classes "electrics" and "non-electrics." To the whole phenomenon of attraction he gave the name "electricity."

Eighty years later, this time in Germany, Otto von Guericke invented a mechanical device that speeded up the production of electricity—a globe made of sulfur, mounted on a shaft, and turned by a crank while the investigator held his hand against it. This rotating globe built up electricity faster and more steadily than the glass-rubbing technique.

Guericke was in the habit of walking around his laboratory, holding his sulfur globe aloft, and driving before it a feather that floated in the air—floated, because it was repelled by the sulfur globe. At other times the globe attracted the feather. Why? Guericke came to the conclusion that it was up to the globe to decide, that "when it does not want to attract, it doesn't attract." Another observation of Guericke's: while he walked through the laboratory with his globe and drove the feather before it, the feather liked to approach "the points of any object whatsoever . . . and it is possible to bring it where it may cling to the nose of any one." He was the first to notice that pointed objects, the human nose included, held a strong attraction for electricity.

Stephen Gray, born in Canterbury, England, in 1666, was a dyer by profession and a talented amateur astronomer. Unusually shy and possessed of a terrible temper, he was also extremely patient. Halfway through his forties he took up residence at the Charterhouse, a home for elderly pensioners, with a shelter for orphan boys nearby; in an unused corner Gray set up a simple laboratory and proceeded to investigate electricity.

It was Gray whose ideas led to an understanding of insulation and conduction. Insulating materials, glass and silk for example, isolate electricity and prevent its free flow. Metals, on the other hand, allow the free flow of electricity and are therefore known as conductors. To learn which substances would serve as conductors, Gray electrified "a Fire-Shovel, Tongs and Poker," an umbrella, a dead rooster, a large map of the world, and a copper teakettle. To demonstrate insulation, he borrowed a child from the orphanage and invented the spectacle of the Dangling Boy. All over Europe, in courts and marketplaces, people copied this performance. Spencer was one of many, although evidently the first who brought the Dangling Boy to America.

In the early eighteenth century a Frenchman, Charles Du Fay, determined that there were two kinds of electricity, "one of which I call vitreous Electricity, and the other resinous Electricity." The first was found in such materials as glass, wool, and animal hair, the second in amber, silk, and paper. This helped explain, or seemed to explain, why the globe and the feather repelled each other. In Du Fay's words, "The Characteristick of these two Electricities is, that a Body of the vitreous Electricity, for Example, repels all such as are of the same Electricity; and on the contrary, attracts all those of the resinous Electricity."

Du Fay brought his student the Abbé Jean-Antoine Nollet to the attention of the French King, Louis XV. Because Nollet (his title, Abbé, designated him as a member of the clergy) was a capable scientist as well as an accomplished and witty lecturer, in 1744 the King chose him as court electrician and instructor in physics to the royal family. In his solemn black robe Nollet moved among the fantastical costumes of Versailles nobles like a crow among peacocks.

By the mid-eighteenth century electrical shows had become popular throughout Europe and were seen even in America, but there was still no earthly use for electricity. And there was no way of storing large quantities of it. It was at this point that the innocent games became serious.

In 1746 Pieter van Musschenbroek, who taught physics at the Dutch University of Leyden, wrote to a colleague:

> I wish to inform you of a new but terrible experiment . . . I am engaged in a research to determine the strength of electricity. With this object I had suspended by two blue silk threads, a gun

ASSEMBLING 148 OF THE KING'S GUARDS,
HE HAD EACH MAN CONNECTED TO THE NEXT.

barrel, which received electricity by communication from a
glass globe which was rapidly turned on its axis . . . From the
opposite end of the gun barrel hung a brass wire, the end of
which entered a glass jar, which was partly full of water. This jar
I held in my right hand, while with my left I attempted to draw
sparks from the gun barrel. Suddenly I received in my right
hand a shock of such violence that my whole body was shaken
as by lightning stroke . . . The arm and body were affected in a
manner more terrible than I can express.

He had invented the world's first device for storing electricity.
Most people called it the Leyden jar, Franklin preferring to call it
Musschenbroek's jar. No matter what it was called, it brought the
smell of mortal danger—and yet it was only a water-filled glass jar, a
few inches in diameter, with a wire inserted into it and held in place
by a cork. Later experimenters wrapped the outside with metal foil,
and many wrapped the inside as well, in both cases increasing the
electrical discharge; others filled the jar with metal shot instead of
water. But it was never more than a glass jar—also called a condenser—that for unknown reasons stored electricity.

The Abbé Nollet explored the effect of the Leyden jar on animals, vegetables, vegetable seeds, and people—especially paralytics
whom he hoped to cure but could not. He was more successful with
a spectacle staged for his royal audience. Assembling 148 of the
King's guards, he had each man connected to the next by holding
the ends of a metal wire between them. A guard at one end grasped
the outside of a charged Leyden jar; when the guard at the other

end touched the central wire, the one inserted into the jar, the current went through the line, transmitted simultaneously from guard to guard, so that all 148 took the shock simultaneously, leaping into the air with stunned amazement on every face.

Franklin and his colleagues knew nothing about this demonstration. News from Europe came to America slowly, spottily, and sometimes not at all. Even when they had a Leyden jar of their own, they were still rubbing a glass tube with buckskin to get the electricity stored in it. Then Philip Syng, one of the Franklinists, invented a labor-saving device to replace the buckskin rubbing: a glass globe mounted on an axle with a small handle attached so that the globe could be turned like a grindstone, while the person turning it held his hand to the globe. Only a few turns were enough to charge up the Leyden jar.

Franklin reported proudly to Peter Collinson, "This we find very commodious, as the machine takes up but little room, is portable, and may be enclosed in a tight box when not in use." He had absolutely no idea that similar devices had existed in England for years, descendants of the one invented by Otto von Guericke.

There was so much he couldn't know—information took six or eight weeks to travel from Europe to America, sometimes much longer. And the more he began to care about these electrical experiments, the more he doubted his own ability to understand them. He was like a man searching for something in a dark room, he said, groping and guessing.

Three months went by before Franklin wrote a second letter to Collinson.

Chapter Three

The King's Picture

O n some days Franklin worked alone;
on others his friends the Franklinists
came to the laboratory and worked

either separately or as a team. It was an informal arrangement. While Franklin was the visionary, the chief and most active researcher, in the early days he wasn't the only one. There were things the Franklinists did as a group that he might never have done alone. Franklin benefited from having like-minded people to egg him on, so that their activities in those early days were a good deal like the doings of schoolboys on summer vacation.

An example is the nonsense of the "magical picture." Imagine a large framed portrait of the English King, George II. Imagine Franklin displaying this portrait on a table and pointing it out to a visitor. "The King," says the visitor, nodding.

Franklin says, "God preserve him," for he has been a lifelong admirer of royalty, and of English kings in particular. As the visitor bends over the picture, he sees that a crown made of gold foil has been placed on the royal head, not directly, but on the glass in front of the portrait. And the top of the frame seems to have been tampered with.

Franklin urges the visitor to remove the King's crown. "Take hold of the frame with one hand," he says, "and with the other hand" endeavor to take off the crown. If there are any other Franklinists present, they, too, recommend removing the little gilt crown—it is designed as a test of loyalty, they say.

The visitor, who knows he is being duped, suppresses a smile and does as he is told, taking hold of the frame with one hand and with the other attempting to—

The moment his hand touches the crown a shock flies through

his body. He lets go of the crown and waits for an explanation—but Franklin is now performing the same maneuver, one hand on top of the frame, the other removing the crown. Apparently Franklin is shock-proof, for nothing happens to him. Because he is a loyal subject, he says.

The visitor demands to know how it was done, and the explanation is complicated—a good deal of time and energy have gone into this magical picture. The glass, the frame, the matting have all been taken apart, gold foil inserted here, here, and here, but none on the exact place on top where the demonstrator had his safe handhold. The secret of the magical picture is that it was made into a sort of Leyden jar—a layer of glass sandwiched between two layers of metal foil.

There were other stunts, large and small. Ebenezer Kinnersley, an unemployed minister and one of the Franklinists, created "a curious machine acting by means of the Electric Fire, and playing Variety of Tunes on eight musical bells." Franklin electrified the iron fence surrounding his house for the amusement of visitors. And as he solemnly announced to Peter Collinson, a practical use for electricity was finally discovered: a way of killing chickens with an electrical charge. When the procedure was tried on some turkeys, the birds were thrown into violent convulsions, then lay as if dead; within fifteen minutes they came groggily back to life. But by using five Leyden jars together Franklin managed to electrocute a ten-pound turkey. "Birds killed in this manner eat uncommonly tender," he maintained, and the chickens, being smaller than turkeys, died quickly, which might "operate as a motive with compassionate persons."

In making these experiments, Franklin found that a man could bear a far greater electrical shock than he had imagined. A letter to his brother John described one such encounter:

> Being about to kill a turkey from the shock of two large glass jars containing as much electrical fire as forty common [Leyden jars], I inadvertently took the whole through my own arms and body, by receiving the fire from the united top wires with one hand, while the other held a chain connected with the outsides of both jars. The company present (whose talking to me, and to one another, I suppose occasioned my inattention to what I was about) say that the flash was very great and the crack as loud as a pistol; yet, my senses being instantly gone, I neither saw the one nor heard the other; nor did I feel the stroke on my hands . . . I then felt what I know not well how to describe, a universal blow throughout my whole body from head to foot, which seemed within as well as without; after which the first thing I took notice of was a violent quick shaking of my body, which gradually remitting, my senses as gradually returned.

He never learned to treat electricity with the respect owed to a dangerous, potentially lethal power. "Too great a charge might, indeed, kill a man," he said, "but I have not yet seen any hurt done by it."

A PRACTICAL USE FOR ELECTRICITY WAS FINALLY DISCOVERED.

The day came when Franklin sat at a writing desk, which in the eighteenth century would have been furnished with an inkwell, sand to dry the ink, a stick of sealing wax, a freshly cut quill pen, some paper, and a candle. He started the letter promised months ago to Peter Collinson:

> In my last I informed you that In pursuing our Electrical Enquiries, we had observed some particular Phenomena, which we lookt upon to be new, and of which I promised to give you some Account; though I apprehended they might possibly not be new to you, as so many Hands are daily employed in Electrical Experiments on your Side the Water.

One was a theory about the nature of electricity, the other a discovery Franklin had more or less stumbled across in his makeshift laboratory—the action of points in what he called the "drawing off" of electrical fire. Because he was unsure about the theory, he left it for later and began with "the wonderful effect of pointed bodies."

Just as he suspected, this was not news on the other side of the water, where points had been a familiar story since Otto von Guericke's time, but it was wonderfully new to Franklin. His account began with a three-inch "iron shot"—a cannonball—that was placed in the mouth of a clean, dry, glass bottle. A piece of cork was suspended nearby, hanging by a silk thread long enough to allow the cork to rest against the shot. When Franklin electrified the shot (touched it with a rubbed glass), there was an immediate effect. The cork was repelled by the shot—shoved away from it so that it stood out at an angle at the end of the thread.

According to Franklin's new and uncertain theory, this was exactly what the cork and the shot were supposed to do. Once the cork touched the electrified shot, it became electrified itself. "Electrified plus," he called it, and two bodies that are electrified plus, or positive, will repel one another.

Taking up a steel needle, he held it about ten inches from the shot and then moved it an inch or so closer. Another inch, and the cork released its pull on the thread and hung down, resting against the shot—it was as if the needle's point had drained out of the shot the electric charge Franklin had given it with the rubbed glass. He tried it again and again; when he tried it at night, the effect was even more striking: "If you present the [steel needle's] point in the dark, you will see, sometimes at a foot distance and more, a light gather upon it, like that of a fire-fly or a glow-worm . . . and at whatever distance you see the light, you may draw off the electrical fire, and destroy the repellency."

And when he fixed a needle to the end of a suspended gun barrel, so that it looked like a miniature bayonet, it became impossible to electrify the gun barrel. No matter how many times a rubbed glass was touched to it, in a darkened room he saw "the fire continually running out silently at the point." This observation, that the electrical fire would run out at the point—would be discharged—was originally made by Thomas Hopkinson, one of the Franklinists, and the germ of it took root in Franklin's mind, ready to spring up later in the form of lightning rods. He wrote to Collinson:

> The doctrine of points is very curious, and the effects of them truly wonderful; and, from what I have observed on experiments, I am of opinion that houses, ships, and even towers and churches may be effectually secured from the strokes of lightning by their means; for if, instead of the round balls of wood or metal which are commonly placed on the tops of weathercocks, vanes, or spindles of churches . . . there should be a rod of iron eight or ten feet in length . . . the electrical fire would, I think, be drawn out of a cloud silently, before it could come near enough to strike . . . This may seem whimsical, but let it pass for the present until I send the experiments at large.

With that he turned to his new theory of electricity, what it was and how it worked. He saw it as a fluid. Rubbing the glass tube gives it an excess of electrical fluid—to be more precise, part of the electrical fluid belonging to the silk rubbing cloth remains on the tube, so it has more than it started with, and the cloth, yes, the cloth . . .

In describing this theory to Collinson, and some of the experiments that led him to it, Franklin seemed tentative, in no great hurry to complete the explanation and finish the letter. Perhaps he was distracted by what he saw from the window—"The vessel is just upon sailing," he wrote, meaning the ship whose captain had agreed to carry his letter across the ocean was making ready to leave. "I cannot [therefore] give you so large an account of American Electricity as I intended." Finishing the letter straightaway, he sanded it to dry the ink, folded it, sealed it with a splotch of melted red sealing wax (the end of the wax stick being held briefly to the candle's flame), and took it at a run to the wharf and the ship.

Long before the letter could have reached London, he frantically wrote another:

> I have lately written two long Letters to you on the Subject of Electricity. On some further experiments since, I have observed a Phenomenon or two that I cannot at present account for on the Principles laid down in those Letters, and am therefore become a little . . . ashamed that I have expressed myself in so positive a manner. In going on with these Experiments, how many pretty systems do we build, which we soon find ourselves obliged to destroy! If there is no other Use discover'd of Electricity, this, however, is something considerable, that it may *help to make a vain Man humble*. I must now request that you would not expose those Letters; or if you communicate them to any Friends, you would at least conceal my Name.

Collinson was a Fellow of the Royal Society, a group of distinguished scientists who served as consultants to the British government. And from the start of their scientific correspondence, Franklin had hoped that Collinson would bring his letters to the attention of the Society, that they might be read aloud at meetings, discussed, even printed in *Philosophical Transactions*, the Society's journal.

For in spite of being a colonial, a printer and publisher on a very small, colonial scale, he expected to be taken seriously by the Royal Society. Because the English believed in fair play they would treat his ideas fairly, in a spirit of impartiality, and this was clear to him much of the time. There were other times, however, when the greatness of that world across the water, where so many worked so diligently, seemed to cast a shadow on the humble sphere to which he belonged.

He formed a plan, at first uncertain, then gradually growing firmer, and centering on the Leyden jar—"that wonderful bottle," he called it, "that miraculous jar." He would find out where it kept the electricity it stored, and in the process achieve a clearer understanding of what electricity was and how it worked.

Chapter Four

The Jar

To find out where the Leyden jar stored its electricity, Franklin began taking it apart so he could analyze the pieces.

He placed a charged jar on a sheet of glass—glass being an insulator, it kept the charge from dribbling away. He removed the cork and the wire, held the jar with one hand, and put a finger of the other hand near the water in the jar. There was a spark, meaning electricity wasn't stored in the cork or the wire.

To analyze the water, he electrified the jar again, placed it on glass, and took out the cork and wire as before. Then he emptied the jar by pouring all its water into an empty bottle that also stood on glass. Taking up that bottle, he expected to get a shock from it, because it was his belief that the electricity was stored in the water. But there was no shock.

Maybe the charge had been lost in the pouring-out process or was still in the first jar, now empty. By pouring fresh water into that first jar—fresh, unelectrified water from Debbie's teapot—he got a shock. Which was unexpected, since it showed that electricity was stored in, of all things, the glass. The glass? Yes, apparently the glass. But was it the shape of the glass, the thickness, or some other quality that mattered? Or was it simply its glassness?

Needing something made of glass, yet different in shape and thickness, he picked up a window pane, laid it flat on his hand, and put a lead plate on top of it so the glass rested between two conducting layers, his hand and the lead. The glass wall of the Leyden jar was likewise sandwiched between two conducting layers of lead foil, inner and outer. He electrified the glass pane, touched the lead plate, and got a shock—so the shape or form of the glass didn't matter, only the glassness did.

Then he put the glass pane between two lead plates that were smaller in circumference than the glass and electrified the glass by electrifying the topmost lead plate. When he removed the glass from between the lead plates, it had no sign of electricity. But when he put the electrified glass between the two lead plates, the top one and the bottom one, he suffered a violent shock. The lead plates were connected through his body. All of this showed, as Franklin wrote, that "the whole force of the bottle, and power of giving a shock, is in the GLASS ITSELF."

He went on to make a discovery that confirmed the half-formed theory he had written about to Peter Collinson, then apologized for. When it was electrified, by way of the wire that entered the water, the Leyden jar became positively charged on the inside—and negatively charged on the outside. Plus in one case, minus in the other. And the two were always equal, both opposite and equal. A moderate plus charge on the inside meant a moderate minus charge on the outside. A big plus charge on the inside meant a big minus charge outside.

Franklin concluded that *when the Leyden jar was charged, one side gained what the other side lost—in exactly the same amount.* And the importance of this observation, the truth he eventually pulled out of it, was that this was the way the physical world worked. The electrical fluid was everywhere, in everything, air, people, animals, objects. It was not created because it didn't have to be created—it was always there. It could be moved about from place to place, but it was eternal and indestructible.

He set out to examine his theory in the laboratory. For no matter how satisfying an idea about electricity might be, until its physical existence was demonstrated it was only an idea, insubstantial as myth. He had to know whether positive charge, negative charge, and the transfer of charge could be demonstrated; in a series of nine experiments that are vividly, sometimes poetically described, Franklin showed the proof. All nine of them were cousins, if not siblings, of an electrical entertainment thought up and carried out by the Franklinists.

The star of this entertainment was a spider with a body of burnt cork, legs of linen thread, and "a grain or two of lead stuck in him, to give him more weight." First, a Leyden jar was placed on insulating wax on a table; the usual wire came out of it, and the linen spider was suspended from that wire by a silk thread. Four or five inches from the jar an upright wire was attached to the table, this wire being as high as the Leyden jar and connected to its outer foil. The spider, in other words, hung at rest between two wires—one connected to the inside of the jar, the other connected to the outside.

But as soon as the jar was electrified in the usual way, the spider could no longer rest. Having no charge itself, it was drawn by the jar's strong positive charge—and flew to the closer wire, the one connected to the inside of the jar.

As soon as it touched that inside wire, the spider itself became charged positively and the two positive charges repelled each other. This sent the spider flying to the wire in the table, the one connected to the outside of the jar. This wire being negatively charged, the spider had only to touch it to be likewise negatively charged and therefore repelled. Like some lunatic of the spider world, it shuttled back and forth, back and forth, with an air of such desperation that some visitors wanted to know how long this could continue, and what the spider ate, and whether he ever slept.

The shuttling between positive and negative ended when equilibrium was finally restored. And it was the spider itself that gradually carried the excess electrical fluid away to the other side, as if that was its mission, the restoration of equilibrium. This equilibrium is the usual state of neutral matter, such as the ground beneath our feet, which can be said to be "in balance." That's why, in spite of our bodies being normally filled with electricity, we never feel electrified.

Ebenezer Kinnersley showed that the Leyden jar could be charged from the outside, through its coat of metal foil, just as well as by way of the hook that led inside to the water. And when the jar was charged in this backward way, the charge on the outside was positive and equal in magnitude to the negative charge on the inside.

It seemed to Franklin that within this simple glass container there existed at one and the same time "a hungry vacuum" demanding to be filled, and a fullness that "presses violently to expand."

"So wonderfully are these two states of Electricity, the *plus* and *minus* combined and balanced in this miraculous bottle! Situated and related to each other in a manner that I can by no means com-

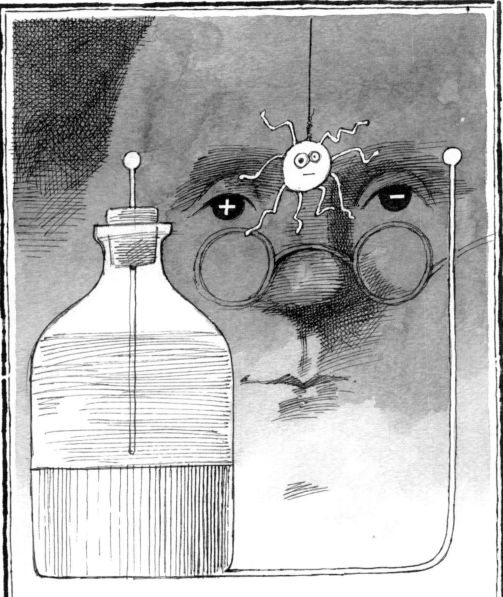

LIKE *SOME LUNATIC OF THE SPIDER WORLD, IT SHUTTLED BACK AND FORTH.*

prehend!" Even if he could not understand it yet, he understood where it led: "There is really no more electrical fire in the [Leyden jar] after what is called its *charging*, than before, nor less after its *discharging*." This discovery came to be called the law of conservation of charge and is considered basic to Franklin's theory of electricity, which can be summed up as follows: Electricity is a fluid; some neutral amount of this invisible fluid is present in all objects, everywhere. Rubbing objects together transfers electrical fluid from one object to another—one object gaining an excess, the other having a shortage. When two bodies with an excess of electrical fluid meet, they repel each other. The same is true for two bodies with a negative supply of fluid. But a positively charged body attracts a neutral one or one negatively charged, because "common matter is a kind of spunge to the electrical fluid." This push-pull of electricity, in which a charge flows from positive to negative and vice versa, is what makes a battery work, its positive and negative poles driving electricity from one side to the other.

While Franklin was working out the proof of his theory, Sir William Watson, an English scientist and member of the Royal Society, was working along roughly similar lines. Franklin eventually learned that Watson had "now discovered and demonstrated . . . that the Electrical Fire is a real Element . . . not created by the Friction, but collected only. In this discovery they were beforehand with us in England, but we had hit on it before we had heard it from them." According to Dr. I. Bernard Cohen, a historian of science and staunch partisan of Franklin's, "Watson is a sort of precursor of

Franklin. But [Watson's] ideas were crude and approximate," more like the Abbé Nollet's than Franklin's.

Although we know that electricity is not an actual fluid, for two centuries the fluid metaphor has been the single most useful way to picture electricity. Students today begin their study of the subject by repeating the demonstrations that Franklin described. Terms he introduced make up our common language of electricity: charge, discharge, condenser, conductor, electrical shock, electrify, minus (negative or negatively), plus (positive or positively), stroke, uncharged, nonconductor.

About his belief that an invisible something is transferred from one body to another during charging, that something turns out to be the negatively charged particle called the electron. Electrons are present in all atoms, therefore in all matter, and rubbing two objects together transfers electrons from one to the other.

Why are electrons considered to be negatively charged? Because Franklin gave the label "positively charged" to glass after rubbing it with a silk cloth. It took 150 more years for experiments by J. J. Thomson, a British physicist, to discover electrons—and then to find that they have a charge opposite to the charge on glass. Thomson won a Nobel Prize for his discovery. In his opinion, "The service which the one-fluid theory has rendered to the science of electricity can hardly be overestimated."

At the end of April 1749, Franklin finished the fourth of his letters to Collinson by confiding that he and the Franklinists were embarrassed at having found nothing in the electrical way that could be useful to mankind. And with "the hot weather coming on, when Electrical Experiments are not so agreeable; 'tis proposed to put an end to them for this Season somewhat humorously in a Party of Pleasure on the Banks of Schuylkill," the river where the "principal people" of Philadelphia had their mansions.

It would be an electrical picnic. Spirits (wine) would be fired (warmed up) by a spark from a Leyden jar located across the river. The spark would travel there by means of a wire suspended from the overhead rope of a ferry's towline, and the return circuit would cross the river "without any other conductor than the water."

A turkey was to be killed for their dinner by electrical shock and roasted on a spit turned by an electrical jack. Then "the healths of all the famous electricians in England, Holland, France, and Germany are to be drank in electrified bumpers." An electrified bumper, Franklin explained, was a thin glass tumbler nearly filled with wine and then electrified so that when brought to the lips it gave a shock, "if the party be close shaved, and does not breathe on the liquor." Because of their sharp points, whiskers might discharge the liquor from a distance, silently robbing it of its power to shock.

Chapter Five

Magically
Magic Squares

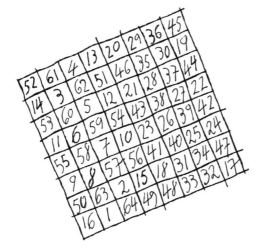

Franklin had been serving since 1736 as clerk of the Pennsylvania Assembly, the colony's lawmaking body.

His duties were to record the details of laws passed and decisions made, and because there were long stretches of time devoted to debate or discussion, sometimes idle discussion known as piffle, a clerk's work could be boring.

It could also be instructive. By the late 1740s, after more than ten years of listening to the Assembly's business, Franklin knew that business as well as he knew his own front door. While other colonies owed their loyalty directly to the Crown, in 1681 Pennsylvania had been awarded by Charles II to the English religious reformer William Penn, who intended it as a "holy experiment," a refuge for Quakers and other persecuted people.

But when Penn died, the colony came under the control of his descendants, known as the Proprietors, and they were not selfless, high-minded, or even Quaker. They lived luxuriously in England and refused to contribute to the defense of the colony—let the colonists defend themselves, they said. This wasn't going to happen. The twelve other colonies raised civilian militias for self-defense, but Pennsylvania's Quakers refused to raise or equip a militia. It was against their pacifist beliefs.

When there was no immediate threat of war, non-Quakers in the Pennsylvania Assembly were content to let the Quaker community follow its principles—"May they long enjoy them," Franklin said. But war inevitably brought changes. Beginning in 1744, King George's War was the North American expansion of the War of the Austrian Succession (involving most of the European nations in a complex web of alliances). Now France and England were the combatants in North America, each with their Indian allies.

In the summer of 1747 French sails appeared in Delaware Bay. They were privateers—not part of the royal navy but privately owned, yet recognized and licensed by their government to attack enemy ships. The privateers raided two plantations, captured a ship coming from the British West Indies, and murdered its captain.

A barrage of rumors from the Indies followed. One of them warned that six French privateers were plotting to join forces in 1748, sail up the Delaware, and sack Philadelphia. The city had no cannons, ammunition, or militia. Most Quakers in the Assembly— although not all—still refused to raise money for weapons. How was the city to defend itself?

"I determined to try what might be done by a voluntary Association of the People," Franklin said. By this he meant an independent militia designed to defend Pennsylvania without help, without so much as a by-your-leave, from the Proprietors. He met with several friends, including the colony's attorney general, to discuss ways and means of carrying out this plan.

Propaganda was the answer they hit on. First, several pieces ran in the *Pennsylvania Gazette* arguing for self-defense. Then a pamphlet appeared, "Plain Truth," written in a style that was typically Franklin—serious argument made digestible by humorous asides: "Till of late, I could scarce believe the Story of him who refused to pump in a Sinking Ship, because one on board, whom he hated, would be saved by it as well as himself."

A series of public meetings followed. Eventually some ten thousand signatures approved the articles of association that

Franklin printed and distributed throughout the colony. The lottery that brought in the money to build a fort below the city and furnish it with cannons, and the getting of those cannons, were largely powered by Franklin. Members of the militia kept a nightly guard among the eighteen-pounders at the fort, and Franklin regularly took his turn of duty there as a common soldier.

For the time being, then, science had to be ushered offstage and into the wings, where it waited for the opportunity to claim center stage again. Yet it was never far from Franklin's consciousness. Far more than a hobby, science was a preoccupation he pursued in various forms from childhood until the end of his life.

Whenever he reached a pause in the day's business, one scientific question or another would patter alluringly across the pathways of his mind, doing its best to distract him. During sessions of the Assembly, as he waited for something worth recording, he began a sort of doodling that evolved into what he called magic squares— one large square divided into smaller squares, each containing a number "disposed in such manner that the sums of every row, horizontal, perpendicular, or [in some cases] diagonal, should be equal." They were not his invention—the name of the original author is lost in the mists of time—but Franklin learned to fill a square of reasonable size pretty much as fast as he could write the numbers down, usually a square of eight, but once of sixteen numbers. He called the latter "the most magically magic of any magic square ever made by any magician."

Franklin was not always proud of his skill with magic squares.

James Logan was a fur trader, a member of the Library Company, and a scholar who knew Latin, Greek, Hebrew, French, and Italian. He was said to be the only person in America who understood Sir Isaac Newton's *Principia Mathematica*. Logan was so impressed by what he had heard of Franklin's magic squares that he told Peter Collinson about them, and Collinson asked Franklin for samples.

The samples were sent, but a week or so later Franklin wrote to Logan, "The magical squares, how wonderful soever they may seem, are what I cannot value myself upon, but am rather ashamed to have it known I have spent any part of my time in an employment that cannot possibly be of any use to myself or others." For the same reason—because it was important to him that his time should be usefully spent—he felt that much of his thinking about science had no particular use. Like the magic squares, it was self-indulgent.

Yet he had been inventing, speculating, dabbling with ideas since boyhood. At the age of eleven, taking oval palettes like those used by painters, he made a set of flippers for hands and feet to help him swim faster. "In swimming," he wrote, "I pushed the edges of these forward, and I struck the water with their flat surfaces as I drew them back . . . I also fitted to the soles of my feet a kind of sandals; but I was not satisfied with them, because I observed that the stroke is partly given by the inside of the feet and the ankles, and not entirely with the soles of the feet." Most youngsters would have noticed only that the sandals didn't work too well, but his analytic eleven-year-old mind needed to find out why.

Some years later, after running away from his apprenticeship, he found himself on his own in London without money and without work. He hoped to meet Sir Isaac Newton, then an old man, but was unable to. He wrote instead to Sir Hans Sloane, secretary of the Royal Society: "I have brought with me [from North America] a purse made of the stone asbestos, a piece of the stone, and a piece of wood . . . called by the inhabitants salamander cotton." Sloane was encouraged to purchase these curiosities; he arranged to meet Ben Franklin, invited the youngster home to Bloomsbury Square, and later bought the North American treasures.

It was on the return voyage that Franklin began a lifelong inquiry into the secrets of the ocean. About a week before landfall the ship snagged some branches of gulfweed, "with which the sea is spread all over, from the Western Isles to the coast of America," he wrote in his journal. One of the branches "bore a fruit of the animal kind, very surprising to see. It was a small shell-fish like a heart." There were some forty of the creatures fastened to that single branch, and when the larger ones opened their shells from time to time they thrust out a set of unformed claws like those of a crab. He called them "vegetable-animals"—we would recognize them as barnacles—and found one very small crab crawling among them.

Would the other vegetable-animals mature into crabs? To find out, he kept the weed in salt water, intending to renew the water every day until they came to shore, but the branch and its fruit soon died. Several days later "we found a flying fish dead under the windlass. He is about the bigness of a small mackerel, a sharp head, a small mouth, and a tail forked somewhat like a dolphin . . . His wings are of a finny substance, about a span long, reaching when close to his body from an inch below his gills to an inch above his tail. When they fly it is straight forward (for they cannot readily turn) a yard or two above the water; and perhaps fifty yards is the furthest before they dip into the water again, for they cannot support themselves in the air any longer than while their wings continue wet." One night Ben sat up late to watch a lunar eclipse, and calculated the ship's longitude by comparing the hour predicted for London to see that same eclipse, and the hour it took place before his eyes. He was twenty years old and the world was fascinating to him.

He was curious about comets, Scottish tunes, the aurora borealis, shells and other remnants of sea life found on mountaintops far from salt water, the earth's magnetism, and the possible shifting of the magnetic poles. He wondered whether dark-colored fabrics grow hot faster in the sun than light-colored ones, and he hoped to learn how ants communicate. He was convinced they did.

In Debbie's kitchen a horde of ants got into a small clay pot filled with molasses. Franklin shook out all but one and hung the pot from a string nailed to the ceiling. When the single ant had eaten as much molasses as it could hold, it made its way up the string to the ceiling, then down the wall to the floor. Within half an hour a swarm of ants appeared, taking the same path to the molasses pot—from the floor to the wall to the ceiling, then down the string to the pot. There they finished off the molasses, and left the way they came. He was certain they had something like speech.

Wanting to know the best routes for connecting one town with another, Franklin first had to know the distance between them, and that was how he came to invent a distance-measuring device, a kind of early odometer, that was attached to the axle of his carriage wheels when he visited post offices.

While living in London many years later, he met a seagoing American relative and learned about the Gulf Stream, a river of water that flows through the Atlantic. From then on, during his several ocean crossings, he made a habit of lowering a thermometer on a string over the ship's side every morning and from two to four times throughout the day. He was almost eighty when he put down, in one place, the rich store of information about the Gulf Stream he had collected during all those years.

To this extraordinary heap of inventions and discoveries, Franklin added a musical instrument known as the glass armonica. During his London years he had attended a concert played on water-filled goblets; they rang when the player struck them with xylophone mallets or rubbed their rims with damp fingers, different notes being produced according to the shape of each bowl and the amount of water in it. He was captivated by the slow, haunting music. Hoping to improve the instrument, he asked a glassblower to make thirty-seven crystal bowls, the largest nine inches in diameter, the smallest three inches, all with holes in the center. The bowls were mounted on a horizontal spindle and played "by sitting before the middle of the set of glasses as before the keys on a harpsichord, turning them with the foot, and wetting them now and then with a spunge and clean water." As he touched the turning edges with wet fingers, the musician produced long, sustained, crystalline notes and chords.

Some four hundred works have been written for the glass armonica, a number of them by Mozart and Beethoven. Marie-Antoinette learned to play the instrument. Dr. Franz Mesmer used it to relax his patients before they were treated by a technique he developed known as mesmerism, or hypnotism. Franklin enjoyed duets with his daughter, Sally, who played the harpsichord while he drew from his armonica "soft warblings rolling smooth and clear." Nowadays, some eight to ten of the instruments are produced each year by a company in Waltham, Massachusetts; they sell for $6,000 to $36,000, depending on size.

Franklin was seventy-eight when he invented bifocals, a pair of glasses in which the upper half is a distance lens, and the lower half is a close-up lens. He found them convenient for traveling because he was able to look through the carriage window at the scenery, and a moment later at a fellow passenger.

By the early months of 1748, King George's War was winding down; soon there would be an uneasy peace, as France and England called off their armies, contenting themselves with sporadic fighting and privateering for the next eight years. Then another costly war would erupt. The two European powers were fighting over immensely valuable possessions in the New World, and in the process both nations came nearer and nearer to bankruptcy.

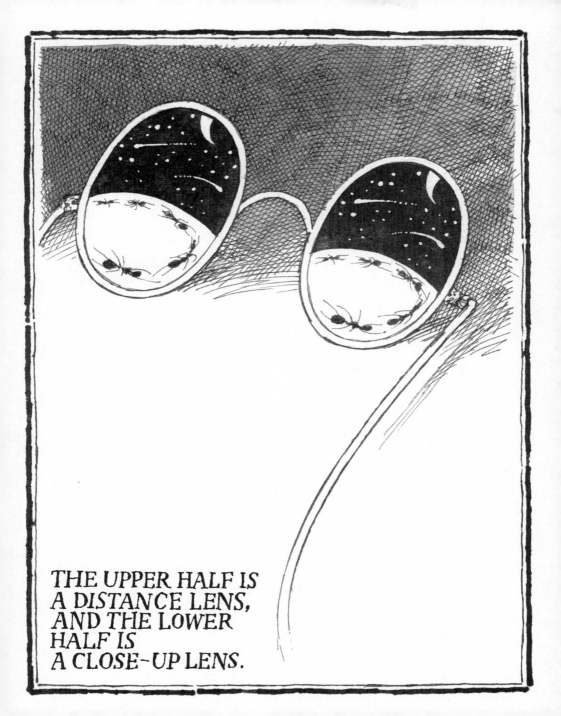

For Franklin the end of hostilities meant he was free to return to experiments. Before doing so he moved his family out of the house on Market Street to one on Race Street, also rented, but in a quieter and somewhat better neighborhood. He was now, at age forty-two, fully and formally retired, the printing business having been placed in the hands of a partner, David Hall, with whom Franklin shared profits and expenses equally. Franklin owned other printing operations, also successful, as well as parcels of land in Philadelphia, and a newly purchased farm in New Jersey. He expected to live well on the income of these properties—not splendidly, but in comfort.

Two slaves, man and wife, were bought for the new house. Franklin had never owned slaves before, although from time to time he had acted as an agent for slave owners, helping them sell their property through the *Pennsylvania Gazette*. "A likely Wench about fifteen years old, has had the Smallpox, been in the Country above a Year and talks English," one notice began. "Inquire of the Printer hereof." Although he lived among Quakers, many of whom had become devout abolitionists by midcentury, Franklin took a cool and slightly scornful attitude toward the institution of slavery; the slaves themselves, he said, were lazy and unreliable. Now, for the first time in his life, he was a slave owner himself.

There was one more change. Franklin had tasted politics. Before, he had only watched while taking notes for the legislature. This time he had conceived a plan, the voluntary association; he had persuaded others to join him, set up a lottery to buy weapons, and bought the weapons. He made the whole enterprise, a complex and uncertain machine, into a working system—it was surely an exhilarating success.

Thomas Penn, one of the colony's two Proprietors, disapproved of the entire affair. He especially disapproved of Franklin, whom he considered "a dangerous man . . . of a very uneasy spirit." Franklin, however, was thinking he might want to seek a seat in the Pennsylvania Assembly.

For William Franklin, life had undergone changes during the same period. He had enlisted in the army, briefly and against his father's advice, and when the episode was over Franklin wrote to his son's grandmother,

> Will Is now 19 Years of Age, a tall proper Youth and much of a Beau . . . He acquired a Habit of Idleness [in the army], but begins of late to apply himself to Business, and I hope will become an industrious Man. He imagined his Father had got enough for him: But I have assured him that I intend to spend what little I have, my self; if it pleases God that I live long enough: And as he by no means wants Sense, he can see by my going on that I am like to be as good as my Word.

He sent the young man to visit relatives in New England, cousins who had been trained as bakers, goldsmiths, and printers, and who knew that William would never have to dirty his hands. He had had the education of a gentleman; he looked like one and

talked like one. Yet people often referred to him as Franklin's illegitimate son, if not his bastard son. Years later John Adams, who became America's second President, called William "an insult to the
morals of America . . . [and] a base-born Brat." Therefore, it was especially important for him to stand straight and tall and hold his
head up.

Settling into the new house on Race Street, the family prepared to be happy there. Debbie had two servants to help her. Sally,
now seven years old, took lessons at dancing school. And Benjamin
Franklin, setting out his electrical equipment, made ready for the
next adventure.

Chapter Six

"Let the experiment be made"

To the ancient world, lightning was a symbol of divine anger or solemn intent. Thunder and lightning accompanied Jehovah's giving of the Ten Commandments on Mount Sinai. Lightning bolts were hurled by Zeus, the chief god of the Greeks. When the Norse god Thor traversed the heavens in his goat-drawn chariot, he made thunder with its rockings from side to side. And the reverence that Europeans paid to the oak is said to arise from the frequency with which it was struck by lightning—chosen by the great sky god above all other trees, it was therefore naturally sacred.

Because lightning inspired terror and the profoundest sense of helplessness, superstitions clustered around it. Mistletoe was said to offer protection; the same was true of embers taken from the Yule log and carefully kept. The ringing of church bells during thunderstorms was widely believed to protect everyone within earshot, and the practice continued in parts of central Europe until the mid-nineteenth century. Some bells bore the Latin for "I break up the lightning."

When storms threatened the German town of Constance, the bells of all the parish churches throughout the countryside were rung. Volunteers climbed the belfries to help the sexton by pulling on bell ropes; some were struck dead by lightning while in the very act of ringing. Nevertheless, citizens of Constance continued to volunteer. In 1784, a German observer pointed out that during the previous thirty-three years, lightning had struck 386 church steeples and killed over a hundred bell ringers.

By the mid-eighteenth century the man in the street was still superstitious about lightning—even about electricity, for that matter, but electricity was created by showmen who were easily avoided, while lightning strikes were unpredictable. In France, the Abbé Jean-Antoine Nollet began a series of popular lectures on physics and electricity with the intention of dispelling "vulgar errors, extravagant fears and faith in the marvelous." In discussing current theories of electricity based on observation rather than superstition, he added that somebody, somewhere, ought to begin experiments proving that electricity and lightning were the same.

The similarity had been seen by experimenters—Stephen Gray, Charles Du Fay, and many others, including Isaac Newton, who touched a needle to a piece of amber that had been rubbed on silk cloth and saw a flame that "putteth me in mind of sheet lightning on a small—how very small—scale." But nobody had ever shown by experiment that electricity and lightning were the same. Nobody had even suggested a way to do it.

Franklin's first ideas on the nature of lightning were more picturesque than useful; ten years earlier he had written a piece for the *Pennsylvania Gazette* explaining that the cause of thunder, lightning, and earthquake was probably the same, and that there could well be thunder and lightning underground, "in some vast repositories." But once he had embarked on his electrical career, the similarity struck him as forcefully as it had the others. Describing how he sent an electric charge through the gilded edges of a book, Franklin spoke of a "vivid flame, like the sharpest lightning." In the next two years he grew increasingly certain of the connection.

A letter in the spring of 1749 offered some tentative observations about lightning storms. Don't take shelter under a tree, he

THE *SIMILARITY* STRUCK HIM
AS *FORCEFULLY AS IT HAD THE OTHERS.*

said, for this has been fatal to many, both men and beasts. "It is safer to be in the open field for another reason," he went on, for standing in the open would allow the rain to soak your clothing—and when clothing is wet, "if a flash in its way to the ground should strike your head, it may run in the water over the surface of your body," but if your clothing is dry the lightning could well go through your body, since blood and other internal liquids are ready conductors.

A few months later he wrote in his journal,

Electrical fluid agrees with lightning in these particulars: 1. Giving light. 2. Colour of the light. 3. Crooked direction. 4. Swift motion. 5. Being conducted by metals. 6. Crack or noise in exploding. 7. Subsisting in water or ice. 8. Rending bodies it passes through. 9. Destroying animals. 10. Melting metals. 11. Firing inflammable substances. 12. Sulphurous smells.—The electrical fluid is attracted by points.—We do not know whether this property is in lightning.—But since they agree in all the particulars wherein we can already compare them, is it not probable they agree likewise in this? Let the experiment be made.

The experiment would be based on the power of points to attract and deflect electrical fire. Iron rods made needle-sharp, and gilded to prevent rust, would be fixed to the outside of a building: "Would not these pointed rods probably draw the electrical fire silently out of a cloud before it came nigh enough to strike, and thereby secure us from that most sudden and terrible mischief!"

On July 29, 1750, Franklin composed a long letter to Collinson. It was a summing-up of his observations about electricity and lightning, as well as a plan for the experiment to prove them. "On the top of some high tower or steeple, place a kind of sentry-box, big enough to contain a man and an electrical stand." The stand would hold one of the sharply pointed iron rods; this rod would bend and pass out the door, then rise upright twenty or thirty feet. Another rod would go from inside the sentry box to the ground. A wire between the tall rod and the one in the ground was to be put in place only in case of a storm—and the purpose of this grounding (the English would call it "earthing") was to channel the electric charge into the earth, where it could do no harm.

"If the electrical stand be kept clean and dry," the letter continued, "a man standing on it when such clouds are passing low, might be electrified and afford sparks, the rod drawing fire to him from a cloud." Here we have an example of the power of points to attract charge: "If any danger to the man should be apprehended (though I think there should be none) let him stand on the floor of his box, and now and then bring near to the rod the loop of a wire that has one end fastened to the leads, he holding it by a wax handle; so the sparks, if the rod be electrified, will strike from the rod to the wire, and not affect him."

This proposal, like everything Franklin had already written to Collinson, was sent in the hope that his English friend would pass it on to the Royal Society, and Collinson did pass it on. Franklin's letter about his single-fluid theory had been read to the Society by

William Watson, who expressed a high opinion of it and claimed the theory was essentially the same as his own.

When Franklin pointed to the similarities between lightning and electricity, that passage, too, was read before the Society, again by Watson. Franklin was flattered when he heard about it. And because Collinson thought so well of the electrical letters as a whole, he offered them to the publisher of the *Gentleman's Magazine*, who decided to put them out in pamphlet form.

The pamphlet was published in the spring of 1751, and two months later Watson read parts of it to the Royal Society—but for some reason he chose not to read the section describing the sentry-box experiment; perhaps he believed it was doomed to failure, and wanted to present the pamphlet in the best possible light. When Franklin learned that Watson had nothing to say about the proposed experiment, he felt that one of his most important ideas was in doubt, that he was being "laughed at by the Connoisseurs," as he said in his autobiography.

His sensitivity to any British criticism was at work here, for the pamphlet was well received by many and had to be reprinted several times to keep up with demand. However, it's also true that no one in England thought of carrying out Franklin's experiment by building an actual sentry box and setting up the lightning rods that would attract electricity, then deflect it harmlessly into the ground.

Chapter Seven

Lightning Electrifies France

Why didn't Franklin build a sentry box himself and carry out his own experiment? The answer is in the first few words of his description:

"On the top of some high tower or steeple." Nowhere in Philadelphia was there a tower sufficiently high, although a spire was planned for Christ Church, and Franklin contributed to the construction fund in the hope of hurrying it along. For the time being the sentry box had to be put aside. It had not occurred to him that a pointed rod of middling height would serve just as well.

He continued his investigations in the upstairs room of the house on Race Street, working pretty much on his own now. One of the Franklinists had died; another, Ebenezer Kinnersley, was touring New England, giving lecture-demonstrations on electricity, touted as "A Piece of Money drawn out of a Person's Mouth in spite of his Teeth, yet without touching it, or offering him the least Violence," and "An extinguished Candle lighted again by a Flame issuing out of Cold Iron." The lectures were so successful that there grew up over the years a belief that all of Franklin's electrical work was stolen from Kinnersley, a belief it was hard to put down, even when Kinnersley himself publicly and strenuously denied it.

In France, the Abbé Nollet's popular lectures offered his own theory involving "effluent flow" and "affluent flow," which in the human body required two sets of pores, one for emitting an electrical fluid, another for taking it in. The theory of the English scientist William Watson was similar to Nollet's, and there were other European researchers who agreed with him. One who did not was Georges-Louis Leclerc, Count de Buffon, a writer, naturalist, and supervisor of the royal gardens. Having come across a French translation of Franklin's pamphlet, Buffon decided to have a better translation made, not only because it was promising work but also because it would embarrass and outclass the Abbé Nollet.

Buffon turned to his friend Thomas François Dalibard, a botanist with a good command of English. Dalibard produced a fresh translation, and just as Buffon had hoped, it mortified the Abbé, who declared that there was no such person as this Franklin, no electrical experiments had been performed in Philadelphia, and it was all an elaborate hoax cooked up by his enemies.

But in the drama of the pamphlet, Nollet was only a sideshow after all, for soon the sentry box itself took center stage, from where it cast its influence over history and politics throughout the Western world.

In France during that period and among people of leisure, there was a passionate interest in science. Men and women alike studied meteorology, astronomy, botany, and chemistry; they took courses at such public and private institutions as the Royal Botanical Gardens and the School of Civil Engineering. And they did it solely for pleasure. Fashionable circles discussed scientific subjects in the evening when they met at fashionable homes; these gatherings were ruled by women, well educated, exquisitely dressed, and charming, for France was not England, where society was ruled by men of noble birth who excelled at shooting birds.

Since the start of the seventeenth century, thinking people all across Europe had been turning their attention to the world around them, eager to find out how it worked. The French differed from other Europeans mainly in the degree of their enthusiasm. It was also true that they made heroes of their philosophers and thinkers; young people wrote personal letters to the philosopher Jean-Jacques Rousseau, addressing him as "Dear Jean-Jacques" and asking him how to live their lives. And all Frenchmen knew that the greatest philosopher in Europe, if not in the world, was their own Voltaire.

With the exception of Nollet and his followers, French men and women of leisure devoured Franklin's pamphlet, discussing it at society gatherings in Paris and at court in the circles closest to the King, Louis XV. Would these experiments work if carried out by others? Would the sentry-box experiment work? Was electricity a genuine force of nature, rather than a curiosity created in the laboratory? And was it true that humans could at long last take command of the heavens by taming the "thunder-gusts"?

When the King expressed a desire to have the Philadelphia experiments performed for him, one of his courtiers, the Duke d'Ayen, offered his château for the occasion. (Some twenty-five years later this same duke would marry off his teenaged daughter to another teenager, the Marquis de Lafayette.) A Monsieur Delor, known as a master of experimental philosophy, was chosen to carry out the demonstrations before the King—the cork spider, the charade of the electrified portrait, Kinnersley's musical machine, and all the other marvels. According to one who was there, "His Majesty saw them with great satisfaction, and greatly applauded Messieurs Franklin and Collinson."

When the performance was over, Dalibard and Delor agreed that the one Philadelphian experiment they had not done was the most dangerous, the likeliest to fail, and yet the most thrilling. They had to do it, there was no resisting the impulse, but they would do it separately, constructing two different sentry boxes in two different places and in total secrecy—to prevent the King's knowing, in case one or both should fail.

Dalibard chose a place called Marly-la-Ville, some twenty-five miles north of Paris. In a walled garden just outside the village he put up a sharply pointed iron rod, an inch or so in diameter and forty feet high. The rod rested on a low wooden platform that rested in turn on insulating supports consisting of four empty wine bottles (this was France after all) held in place by ropes fastened to three huge wooden supports.

A wooden shelter just large enough to contain a man was built around the base of the rod, and an old soldier named Coiffier was assigned to duty there—instructed to guard the sentry box at all times and, in case of a storm, to carry out certain instructions without regard to his own welfare or safety. (Dalibard seems to have approached the experiment with caution, appointing someone else to take the physical risk.)

On May 10, 1752, at about two in the afternoon, the soldier Coiffier sensed an approaching storm—dark clouds, a little rain, an ominous rumble of thunder. Following instructions, he entered the sentry box and picked up a long brass wire by its insulated handle. The storm came nearer; he touched the wire to the iron rod. Sparks! A stink of sulfur! A loud sizzle and crackle in the air! Terrified, he dropped the wire and shouted for the village priest. Sparks and a sulfurous smell could be electricity, but could equally well be the Devil. (The odor actually came from ozone, a by-product of electrical discharge.)

The priest, having heard the thunder, set out at a run, several villagers running behind him. The villagers, seeing what a great hurry their priest was in, concluded that Coiffier was dead, killed by thunder, for it was widely believed that thunder, rather than lightning, was the killer. Soon they had called out the rest of the village to mourn poor Coiffier.

As the rain turned to hail, the priest arrived; seeing there was no danger, he took hold of the wire. Six times he held it to the iron rod, drawing sparks each time; then he kept the wire and rod in place for the duration of a Lord's Prayer and a Hail Mary. He never noticed the bruises on his arm, or the strong smell of sulfur on his clothing, both of which startled people he met as he rushed home. There the priest wrote a hurried letter to Dalibard, and sent Coiffier off to deliver it: "I am announcing to you, Monsieur Dalibard, what you have been waiting to hear: the experiment is finished . . . I performed it six times in about four minutes, in the presence of several people." He would have continued, he said, but the storm died down.

A few days later, in Paris, Delor performed his own version of the experiment. Using an iron rod ninety-nine feet high, he drew off an abundance of sparks during a thunderstorm.

Dalibard then wrote to France's Royal Academy of Sciences: "M. Franklin's idea has ceased to be a conjecture, here it has be-

THEN HE KEPT THE WIRE AND ROD IN
PLACE FOR THE DURATION
OF A LORD'S PRAYER AND A HAIL MARY.

come a reality." The news reverberated throughout the kingdom. Who is this Monsieur Franklin? the French wanted to know. Could it be true that he was neither English nor German, but of all things a colonial in that distant land where people clung to the edge of a wilderness? And not trained in science, but rather—this was especially strange—a retired printer?

Louis XV ordered that an expression of grateful thanks be sent to Mr. Franklin; it was posted to Peter Collinson, who forwarded it to Philadelphia. And while the King's words journeyed across the ocean under billowing sails, the sentry-box experiment was performed by three scientists in England and two in Germany, as well as by a Dr. le Monnier, the French King's physician, all successfully. Franklin was famous throughout Europe, but until the ship bearing the King's letter sailed into port at Philadelphia, he knew nothing about it. He had no reason to suspect that people speaking several different languages recognized his name; discussed him; praised, admired, and marveled at him.

Chapter Eight

The Puzzling Kite

News of the triumph at Marly-la-Ville traveled all the way to Russia, a vast and exotic land hardly known to most Europeans.

The Emperor Peter the Great had made attempts to modernize the country, to create a window to the West; he had an Academy of Sciences built in St. Petersburg and opened it in 1725, but no Russians were able to pass the entrance examinations, and the first student body of eight had to be imported from Germany.

When St. Petersburg heard about the success of the sentry-box experiment, one of those who responded was a Swedish-born professor of physics, Georg Richmann. He built what he called a "thunder-machine" for his house—the name persisted, even among those who knew perfectly well they were investigating lightning, not thunder. This machine was a copy, more or less, of the sentry-box design at Marly—but in what proved to be a fatal error, Richmann neglected to provide an insulated platform.

The following account is taken from Franklin's *Pennsylvania Gazette*, March 15, 1754: One day in the summer of 1753, when he was at the St. Petersburg Academy preparing a speech, Richmann happened to look out the window and saw a thundercloud coming from the north. He started immediately for home, accompanied by a friend, M. Sokolaw. They heard distant thunderclaps and noted that there was not a drop of rain.

At home, Richmann stationed himself next to his thunder-machine and prepared to carry out some experiments with an electrical needle and a vessel of water partly filled with brass filings. He "stood about a Foot from the Bar, attentively observing the Needle. Soon after M. Sokolaw saw . . . a Globe of blue and whitish Fire, about four inches diameter, dart from the Bar against M. Richmann's Forehead, who fell backwards without the least outcry. This was succeeded by an Explosion like that of a small Cannon." A thick smoke invaded the room as Sokolaw ran for help.

A surgeon came to examine Richmann, who was entirely lifeless; he had been killed quickly, and probably painlessly, by electrical shock from his apparatus. A cherry-red spot was clearly visible on his forehead. The electric force of the "thunder" had passed out of his body and into the floorboards, leaving his feet and fingers blue and one shoe torn but only partly burned.

The *Gazette's* story ends with some remarks by Franklin: "The new Doctrine of Lightning is, however, confirmed by this unhappy Accident; and many Lives may hereafter be saved by the Practice it teaches." Because Richmann's rod and wires were not grounded—and because Richmann himself was standing too near the end of the wire—he "helped with his Body to compleat that Communication." If the wire had gone from the roof directly into the earth, neither the house nor any of the family could have been injured.

Franklin's own encounter with the electricity of a summer storm had taken place a year earlier, probably in June of 1752, when he flew his famous kite. This date is not entirely certain, however. Months went by before he said anything about it, whether to readers of the *Gazette* or *Poor Richard's Almanac*, or to Peter Collinson. Even in August, when Louis XV's letter arrived in Philadelphia, Franklin said nothing.

There is no firsthand account of the kite-flying—not in Franklin's autobiography, letters, or journal. Most of what we know about it comes by way of Joseph Priestley, a distinguished English chemist, the co-discoverer of oxygen, and a longtime friend of Franklin's—and Priestley told the story in *The History and Present State of Electricity*, written some fifteen years after the event.

Another remarkable aspect of the kite experiment: Franklin knew he would be collecting an electrical charge of unknown size, possibly tremendous, since huge amounts of charge can accumulate in the upper atmosphere; they are capable of killing in an instant, and Franklin knew it. He also knew the safe procedure would require the grounded metal rod in an empty place. Perhaps he was so accustomed to being knocked out, then getting up and dusting himself off, that he couldn't take seriously the chance of being fatally struck by lightning.

Some biographers maintain that the kite experiment was an example of one man's courage in challenging nature. But if he had truly acknowledged the risks, would he, a good father, have taken William along?

Priestley's account begins when Franklin realized there was no need to wait until the spire went up on Christ Church: "It occurred to him that by means of a common kite he could have better access to the regions of thunder than by any spire whatever." Priestley goes on to say that Franklin made a small cross of two light strips of cedar, with arms long enough to reach to the four corners of a large, thin silk handkerchief. After tying the corners of the handkerchief to the ends of the cross, he had the body of a kite, to which he added a tail, a loop, and a length of twine. At the top of the cross he fixed a sharp, pointed wire to attract electric fire. And at the end of the twine, next to the handhold, he tied a silk ribbon, with a key fastened to the place where twine and silk were joined. If lightning truly was electricity, then the fire attracted by the pointed wire would travel down the kite string in the form of sparks, and the sparks would end up at the key in Franklin's hand.

Priestley's account continues: At the first hint of a coming thunderstorm, Franklin set off for a walk. But "dreading the ridicule which too commonly attends unsuccessful attempts in science," he told nobody about it except William, who went with him; his son was then in his early twenties. Together they walked into a field in which there was a shed convenient for his purpose, and there they raised the kite. A good deal of time went by without its being electrified, and Franklin considered giving up—until he noticed some loose threads on the string. They were trying to stand erect, seeming to avoid one another. "Struck with this promising appearance, he immediately presented his knuckle to the key," Priestley tells us, "and . . . the discovery was complete. He perceived a very evident electric spark." There were more sparks, even before the string was thoroughly wet, and when the rain had wet it all the way through "he collected electric fire very copiously."

Priestley read the passage about the kite experiment to Franklin while his *History and Present State of Electricity* was still in manuscript, which explains the many intimate details he could have got only from the story's central character—and all the same, one wonders why Franklin published nothing about the kite until

October 1752. And why he told nobody, not even Ebenezer Kinnersley, who was lecturing on electricity in Philadelphia during the month of September.

It was William, and only William, who knew the story from the start. He, too, was fascinated by electricity, although not to the same degree as his father; William had charted the course of a lightning bolt that struck a house in Philadelphia, following its trail through the house inch by inch, and concluded that instead of taking the shortest route, it made detours to touch metal fixtures at several points. His father was pleased with William's observations, pleased altogether with the young man William had become.

On October 19, in a letter to Peter Collinson, Franklin finally told the story of the kite, but in a tone that was strangely impersonal: "As frequent mention is made in public papers from Europe of the success of the Philadelphia experiment [at Marly-la-Ville] for drawing the electric fire from clouds . . . it may be agreeable to the curious to be informed that the same experiment has succeeded in Philadelphia, though made in a different and more easy manner." Nowhere does the letter suggest that Franklin had anything to do with this experiment.

On that same date, October 19, the *Pennsylvania Gazette* carried the first American news of the kite, and here again the style was cool, impersonal. Poor Richard had something additional to tell in the *Almanac*, something of great significance that Franklin had waited until then to reveal: "It has pleased God in His goodness to mankind, at length to discover to them the means of securing their habitations and other buildings from . . . thunder and lightning. The method is this: Provide a small iron rod (it may be made of the rod-iron used by nailers) but of such length that, one end being three or four feet in the moist ground, the other may be six or eight feet above the highest part of the building. To the upper end of the rod fasten about a foot of brass wire the size of a common knitting-needle, sharpened to a fine point."

About the mysteries surrounding the story of the kite, one explanation is offered by the biographer Carl Van Doren: "Can Franklin deliberately have kept his secret till October so that he might publish at the same time . . . in his newspaper and in his almanac the two most important pieces of his year's news?" Van Doren is referring to the kite experiment and the invention of the lightning rod, and he finishes by saying, "That is what he did."

In September of 1753, Franklin put up his own lightning rod, which extended some nine feet above the chimney of his Race Street house. From it came a wire that went down through the staircase to the pump of a well, where it was grounded. "On the staircase opposite to my chamber door the wire was divided; the ends separated about six inches, a little bell on each end; and between the bells a little brass ball suspended by a silk thread, to play between and strike the bells when clouds passed with electricity in them." Franklin drew charges for his experiments from the separation between the ends of the wire.

One night he was awakened by loud cracks on the staircase. Opening the door, he saw that instead of vibrating as usual between

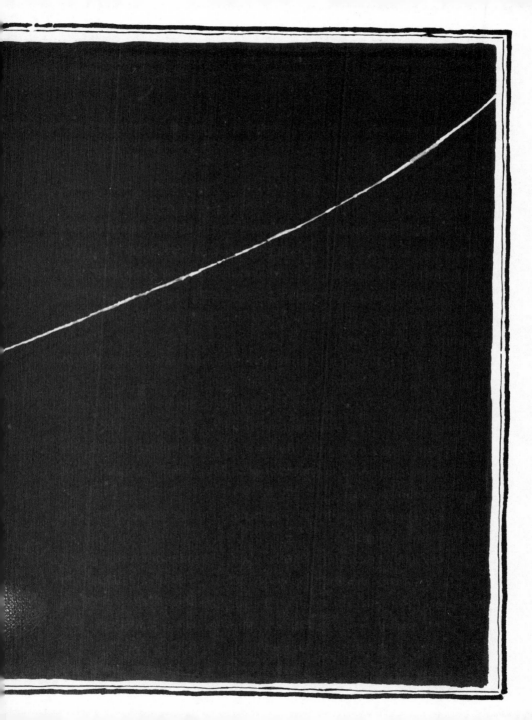

the two bells, the brass ball was repelled—kept at a distance from both of them—while electric fire passed between them in a dense, white stream, more or less continuous, and seemingly as large around as a finger, "whereby the whole staircase was inlightened as with sunshine, so that one might see to pick a pin."

Eventually 1752, the triumphant year of Marly and lightning rods, gave way to 1753, without any expressions of jubilation on Franklin's part. He left no hints about how he felt, no marveling at what had been accomplished. Perhaps there were letters that no longer survive; perhaps his feelings were spoken but never recorded. There is a wistful note to his brother John in January 1753, wishing him a happy new year and inquiring about an old-fashioned clock that had been in the family for years: "It had I remember a sweet Bell . . . You have never mentioned anything to me of my Electrical Papers. So I conjecture you have either not had time to read them, or do not like them."

It was only in April, more than half a year after receiving Louis XV's letter, that Franklin allowed himself to rejoice—and even then he was tentative about it, unsure whether or not he ought to be joking:

The "Tatler" tells us of a Girl, who was observed to grow suddenly proud, and none could guess the Reason, till it came to be known that she had got on a new pair of Garters. Lest you should be puzzled to guess the Cause, when you observe any thing of the kind in me, I think I will not hide my new Garters under my Petticoats, but take the Freedom to show them to you, in a Paragraph of our Friend Collinson's last Letter . . . On reconsidering this Paragraph, I fear I have not so much Reason to be proud as the Girl had; for a feather in the Cap is not so useful a Thing, or so serviceable to the Wearer, as a Pair of Good Silk Garters. The Pride of Man is very differently gratified, and had His Majesty sent me a Marshal's Staff, I think I should scarce have been so proud of it as I am of your Esteem.

The letter was written to Jared Eliot, a clergyman, physician, farmer, and writer on agricultural matters. Otherwise, little is known about Franklin's reaction to the news that the experiment he designed had been performed for the French court, that it had succeeded nobly, and that he was now a hero in France, applauded by the King, known and admired everywhere in Europe.

In the summer of 1753, Harvard University awarded Franklin the honorary degree of master of arts, the first ever granted to anyone not a member of Harvard's faculty. Yale did the same. St. Andrews University in Scotland gave him the honorary degree of doctor of laws. And in 1762 Oxford University voted to award him the same degree, an honorary doctorate of law, whenever he would be pleased to visit the university; he did so in April of that year, and was honored elaborately in Latin, while at the same time William was made a master of arts for his help with the kite experiment.

In 1753 the Royal Society awarded Franklin the Copley Medal, England's most distinguished prize for science; he was the first person living outside of Britain to receive it. Three years later the Society made him a Fellow, so that if he wished, he might write F.R.S. after his name, meaning Fellow of the Royal Society. (He never did.) Some years later he became a member of the Society's Council, and in 1772 was appointed to the French Royal Academy as a foreign member.

In America, recently, a federal interagency group surveyed the types of buildings and facilities endangered by lightning: they range from homes and skyscrapers to missile bases and nuclear power plants. "The conclusions of the Federal Interagency Lightning Protection User Group are: That Franklin, or conventional, lightning protection systems . . . are highly effective in preventing lightning damage."

The success of Franklin's lightning-rod system was not always apparent, however. In the years just before the outbreak of the American Revolution a controversy developed between the "blunts" and the "points"—those who believed in blunt lightning rods and those who believed in pointed ones. And because Franklin was identified with the points, King George III wanted nothing to do with them.

The story goes that the King sent for the president of the Royal Society—Sir John Pringle, a good friend of Franklin's. The King asked Pringle to persuade the Society to switch its approval from points to blunts. Pringle replied that His Majesty could change the law of the land but was powerless to change the laws of nature.

In that case, the King said, he would appoint someone else

as president of the Royal Society, and Pringle was compelled to resign.

A little poem became popular in England during that period:

> While you, great George, for safety hunt,
> And sharp conductors change for blunt,
>   The nation's out of joint:
> Franklin a wiser course pursues,
> And all your thunder fearless views,
>   By keeping to the *point*.

Chapter Nine

A Change of Direction

In his long life, Franklin spent only six years, from 1746 to 1752, as a full-time scientist. Yet this shortened career wasn't what he had in mind when he campaigned successfully for a seat in the Pennsylvania Assembly. He expected to continue his experiments, and since the Assembly met only a few months in the year and he was already retired from business, the rest of the time was surely his to do with as he pleased—read, philosophize with friends, and explore further into the mysteries of electricity.

But it wasn't possible, or at any rate not possible for him, and the reason seems to have been his deep-seated belief that science was a pleasure, a luxury, while public life, especially in difficult times, was far more important than the desires of one individual: "Had Newton been Pilot but of a single common Ship, the finest of his Discoveries would scarce have excused . . . his abandoning the Helm one hour in Time of Danger."

When Franklin took his Assembly seat, in 1751, England and France were supposedly at peace, but the peace was more like an armed truce. Recent French incursions into the Ohio Valley signaled the start of another war, or else the resumption of the earlier one. By 1756 the new conflict would become the French and Indian War, a seven-year contest for mastery of the North American continent. Both England and France pursued alliances with various Indian tribes, whose loyalty shifted from one side to the other, according to which nation offered a better chance of survival.

In 1754 Britain called a conference in Albany, New York, to consider an intercolonial treaty with the Iroquois, an idea that could have been put forward by Franklin himself. The "intercolonial" part was what appealed to him. America's first-ever political

cartoon—drawn by Franklin and published in his *Pennsylvania Gazette*—showed a snake chopped into eight parts, each part marked with the initials of one of the eight northern colonies. Beneath it were the words "Join, or Die."

He attended the conference as a commissioner sent by the Assembly, with his son William as his aide. Together they met Indian sachems and delegates from other colonies, but for Franklin the important business was not the Iroquois or even the French, but union. He had brought his pamphlet "Short Hints Towards a Scheme for Uniting the Northern Colonies," although he doubted any of the colonies were likely to approve it. They were too different in their interests, he said, too suspicious of one another.

Before the colonies could approve or disapprove, the plan was voted down by the British, in Franklin's opinion because "it was judged to have too much of the democratic." Yet he kept faith with it; his ideas developed further over time, but there were always those same two elements—the united colonies, robust and flourishing, and wise, principled Mother England. Bound together in an English-speaking commonwealth, they had the potential to become, in Franklin's words, "the greatest Political Structure Human Wisdom ever created."

But for this to happen, the colonies must first push aside petty quarrels and unite. Franklin's appointment as deputy postmaster-general for North America was gratifying because of the money it brought, and the opportunity for placing relatives in a considerable variety of positions (William as postmaster of Philadelphia, the place his father was vacating, to be succeeded by Joseph Read, a relation of Debbie's, then by Peter Franklin, while John Franklin became postmaster in Boston, succeeded by his widow). There was another advantage to Franklin's new position: he would be able to visit every one of the thirteen very separate colonies and see for himself what they had in common and how they might one day be brought together.

The Albany Conference of 1754—later called the Albany Congress—marked his entry into a new life and a new incarnation of himself as politician and statesman. This change of direction began with the retelling of an old story, Pennsylvania's need to defend itself. French-sponsored Indians had attacked settlers all along the northern frontier; whole families were scalped within ninety miles of Philadelphia. Once again the Assembly battled the Proprietors, those stiff-necked descendants of William Penn who lived in England and controlled the colony. The outbreak of war had increased the need for men and money, but once again the Quakers refused to send men into combat, while the Penns would not pay taxes.

By now the Assembly had to admit that pressure from a distance of three thousand miles would never move the Penns. Someone would have to cross the ocean and set things right—remove the colony from the hands of the Proprietors and put it where it belonged, in the hands of the King, so that taxes could be levied and paid, and the colony enabled to defend itself. In February of 1757 Franklin wrote to William Strahan, his longtime correspondent and fellow printer, "Our Assembly talk of sending me to England speedily. Then look out sharp, and if a fat old fellow should come to your printing house and request a little smouting [freelance printer's work], depend upon it 'tis your affectionate friend and humble Servant, B. Franklin."

Five years had passed since the lightning-rod experiment at Marly-la-Ville, and Franklin, once a Philadelphia businessman, was now a Fellow of the Royal Society with an international reputation. Pennsylvania could send him to the English court without fear that he—and they—would be laughed at, while supporters of the Penns were delighted with the prospect of Franklin's being out from under foot for several months, on a mission they believed was sure to fail.

He made out his will, gave Debbie a power of attorney, and left Philadelphia for New York with William. There they boarded their ship and spent three weeks waiting for the captain to decide he was ready to sail. Sally came along to spend part of the waiting time with her father, and together they went sightseeing. If she had been a boy her father would surely have taken her with him, but a girl of thirteen needed her mother, and no earthly power could compel Debbie to set foot on that ship, much less cross an ocean in it.

William could hardly wait. His father had enrolled him, a few years earlier, at one of the Inns of Court in London to study law. The city would give him polish. He would be called to the bar there, set up in practice, marry. Franklin would see to everything.

For Franklin himself, the opportunity to "go home" was the fulfillment of a youthful dream: London offered symphonies, museums, theaters, and grand libraries—none of which could be had in Philadelphia, or anywhere in America. At long last he would come face-to-face with Peter Collinson; together they would attend meetings of the Royal Society. He would see the King, although from a great distance. Franklin regarded the King with a mixture of awe and affection, and had never even thought of America's being set adrift—cut off from its ties to the Mother Country.

Certain aspects of England were especially important to him, such as the right of Englishmen, even the poorest and most ignorant of them, to a trial by jury. The right to petition the King, to be secure in one's property, to be taxed only by one's own elected representatives. Commonly known as "English liberties," these rights had no equivalent in France, for example, or the German states, and were justly envied there. And since citizens of the thirteen colonies were as English as anyone living in England, they were protected by English liberties.

It was unfortunate that Sally couldn't come, or Debbie. But father and son would not be gone for long, and they had Peter and King to look after them—King belonged to William, Peter to Franklin. Peter's wife, Jemima, stayed behind. Among the legal matters Franklin had arranged before departure were instructions for freeing Peter and Jemima in the event of their owner's death.

As for Debbie, she was suffering from a bad cold, fever, and feelings of weakness. As she wrote to a friend, she was "very weak indeed . . . not able to bear the least thing in the world."

Her husband expected to be gone only a few months. Neither of them could know that, except for a two-year interval, he would be away for seventeen years.

Part II
At Large in the World

Chapter Ten

Pennsylvania's Man in London

The two Franklins, William and his father, arrived in London in late July 1757 to find a city in the full bloom of midsummer.

A happy fate brought them to lodgings at Number 36 Craven Street, close to the Parliament buildings and Whitehall, and not far from the home of the Royal Society, Crane Court, off Fleet Street.

Their landlady, a widow by the name of Margaret Stevenson, became Franklin's almost-sister, and her eighteen-year-old daughter, Polly, became his godchild. They introduced him to the London shops, overflowing with the treasures of the world, and the man who invented Poor Richard sent cratefuls of booty across the ocean to Debbie: shoes, pins, gloves, saucepans, carpeting, bedding, a large-print Common Prayer Book so she might be "reprieved from the Use of Spectacles in Church," and enough fabric to make a fine gown. He wrote to her in detail:

A crimson satin cloak for you, the newest fashion . . . Seven yards of printed Cotton, blue ground to make you a Gown; I bought it by Candlelight and liked it then, but not so well afterwards; if you do not fancy it, send it as a present from me to Sister Jenny. There is a better gown for you of flowered Tissue, sixteen yards, of Mrs. Stevenson's Fancy, cost 9 Guineas; and I think it a great Beauty . . . I also forgot among the China to mention a large fine Jugg for Beer, to stand in the Cooler . . . I fell in Love with it at first Sight for I thought it looked like a fat jolly Dame, clean and tidy, with a neat blue and white Calico gown on . . . good natured and lovely, and put me in mind of— Somebody.

There were moments of homesickness, but in the excitement of London they tended to melt away.

And Debbie? She did her best to keep busy. She helped at the hospital, caring for a stranger stricken with smallpox—he sent her some fish by way of thanks—and lost sleep because of the bells on her husband's lightning conductor. He told her to "tie a piece of Wire from one Bell to the other, and that will conduct the lightning without ringing or snapping, but silently. Though I think it best the Bells should be at Liberty to ring."

Peter Collinson presented himself the first day after Franklin's arrival. He was followed by a succession of scientists, politicians, merchants with interests in America, as well as society people—not from the topmost level but from the high middle. Franklin bought silver knee buckles for his breeches, and fitted in. He loved London, loved the English people: "Why should that petty island, which compared to America is but like a stepping-stone in a brook . . . why, I say, should that little island enjoy in almost every neighborhood more sensible, virtuous, and elegant minds than we can collect in ranging a hundred leagues of our vast forests?" Cushioned by the kindness and comfort of Craven Street, he was intensely happy that first year.

But when it came to the Penns, nothing budged. For six months he was unable even to meet them, all his dealings being with their lawyer. He learned to lobby, making his views known to people in a position to help—which meant in practice wining and dining in London society, six nights a week. He enjoyed it and learned from it, developing a habit of quiet observation in the company of strangers.

By 1760 it was decided by the Privy Council (a group of noblemen acting as advisers to the King) that England would tax developed lands owned by the Penns, but not the far greater unsurveyed tracts. Half a loaf being better than none, Franklin could have gone home at that point, but he stayed. Apart from his enjoyment of the city and its people, there was a practical reason. For some time he had been involved in a scheme for new settlements beyond Pennsylvania's Allegheny Mountains. William had also invested in it; like many others, both father and son hoped to make their fortunes there. It would take time and patient persuasion, however, which could be spent far more effectively in London than in Philadelphia.

The day came when William was finished with his studies; having put on a black robe and been called to the bar at Westminster Hall, he was a lawyer now. William Strahan considered him "one of the prettiest young gentlemen" from America it was ever his pleasure to meet—the two Franklins, father and son, went everywhere together, Strahan said; they were easy and intimate companions, they were like brothers.

And now that William was ready to assume his place in the world, he must have a wife. In his heart of hearts his father had already chosen one: Polly Stevenson, his landlady's daughter. Remarkably well educated, blessed with a lively mind and a charming sense of humor, she was also prim, proper, and dutiful. Franklin called her "my dear good Girl."

Because she lived with an aunt in Kensington (it was assumed that Polly would one day inherit the aunt's fortune), she was at home in Craven Street only for visits. One day she begged Franklin to correspond with her—not aimlessly, she said, but with a view to teaching her "natural Philosophy," meaning science. It was an expression of genuine interest on her part, but also of a fatherless girl's desire to win the approval of a man she greatly admired.

He began by sending the first volumes of a science series intended for young people: "I would advise you to read with a Pen in your Hand," he said, "and enter in a little Book short Hints of what you find that is curious or may be useful; for this will be the best Method of imprinting such Particulars in your Memory." Some of the curiosities would be useful in themselves; others would serve at least "to adorn and improve your Conversation." Surely this was the way Franklin had gone about educating himself.

He further advised Polly to keep a good dictionary on hand and immediately look up any word she failed to understand. When a point occurred in which "you would be glad to have farther Information than your Book affords you, I beg you would not in the least apprehend that I should think it a Trouble to receive and answer your Questions. It will be a Pleasure and no Trouble."

In the letters that followed, Polly asked about the lives of insects, about the tides, evaporation, the workings of barometers, and how different colors absorb heat. Franklin always answered at length, patiently, appreciatively: " 'Tis a very sensible question you ask." He outlined simple experiments: "Walk but a quarter of an

Hour in your Garden when the Sun shines, with a Part of your Dress white, and a Part black; then apply your Hand to them alternately, and you will find a very great Difference in their Warmth. The Black will be quite hot to the Touch, the White still cool."

He recalled an experiment he had done years ago:

I took a number of little Square Pieces of Broad Cloth from a Taylor's Pattern Card, of various Colours . . . Black, deep Blue, lighter Blue, Green, Purple, Red, Yellow, White . . . I laid them all out upon the Snow in a bright Sunshiny Morning. In a few Hours (I cannot now be exact as to the Time) the Black being warmed most by the Sun was sunk so low as to be below the Stroke of the Sun's Rays; the dark Blue almost as low, the lighter Blue not quite so much as the dark, the other Colours less as they were lighter; and the quite White remained on the Surface of the Snow, not having entered it at all.

From this he drew almost a dozen homely and practical conclusions, most having to do with the importance of wearing white in the sun, because it will not absorb heat—"What signifies Philosophy that does not apply to some Use?"

In his correspondence with Polly, Franklin appears at his most endearing—generous, wise, affectionate. Having come to love her and value her friendship, it seemed natural to want her for his daughter-in-law. But in 1762, thanks to his father's connections, William was named Royal Governor of New Jersey, and then, without any help from his father, he chose a bride: Elizabeth Downes, the daughter of a Barbados sugar planter. Her manners were elegant, her disposition pleasant. She had had the narrow education usual for English gentlewomen—music, dancing, French, arithmetic, writing—without any attempt at philosophy or history. But this was hardly her fault. Although he never took an interest in her, never tried to charm or instruct her, Franklin had no complaint against Elizabeth. It was the marriage that hurt him, that did him an injury from which his affection for William never fully recovered.

Perhaps the root of the injury was William's making such a decision on his own—taking control of his life rather than following tamely where his father led. There was another complication. Two years earlier William had learned he had an infant son, the mother unknown except to him. Instead of taking the baby into his household, acknowledged as his own, William found foster parents to care for him. The child was given the name William Temple Franklin, to be known as Temple. When he was brought to Craven Street for a visit, Franklin told Polly and Mrs. Stevenson that the boy was the offspring of a distant relative.

In the summer of 1762, only three short weeks before William's wedding at a fashionable London church, Franklin sailed for home. Just before leaving, he sent a brief note to Polly:

> This is the best Paper I can get at this wretched Inn, but it will
> convey what is intrusted to it . . . It will tell my Polly how much
> her Friend is afflicted that he must, perhaps never again, see

PERHAPS THE ROOT OF THE INJURY WAS
WILLIAM'S MAKING SUCH A DECISION ON
HIS OWN — TAKING CONTROL OF HIS LIFE
RATHER THAN FOLLOWING TAMELY
WHERE HIS FATHER LED.

one for whom he has so sincere an Affection . . . whom he once flattered himself might become his own in the tender Relation of a Child; but can now entertain such pleasing Hopes no more. Will it tell *how much* he is afflicted? No, it cannot. Adieu, my dearest Child: I will call you so; why should I not call you so, since I love you with all the Tenderness, all the Fondness of a Father?

There is no record of what either Polly or William thought of the match Franklin had wanted so intensely to bring about.

Back in Philadelphia, he was welcomed, fussed and exclaimed over by a seemingly endless procession of well-wishers. They came to his home, they met him on the street or in the coffeehouse, they told him that in his absence he had been reelected to the Pennsylvania Assembly five years in a row. But when he went before the Assembly to give an accounting of his expenses in London, there were members who claimed he had lived extravagantly, cheating, lying, embezzling, and accomplishing very little. Some were jealous of Franklin's successes. Others resented the rise to power of his illegitimate son. John Penn, the son of one Penn and nephew of another, called the choice of New Jersey's Governor "a shameful affair," a dishonor and disgrace. This same young Penn was slated to become Governor of Pennsylvania.

But in spite of Penn's influence, and in spite of his many other detractors, the Assembly voted Franklin a retroactive salary for his work in England.

After a long and uncommonly stormy voyage, William and his bride arrived from London. Leaving Elizabeth with Debbie to recuperate, father and son went off to New Jersey for the swearing-in ceremony that would transform William into a Royal Governor. There were fifteen days of speeches, dinners, and meetings with dignitaries, then an inspection of the Governor's mansion at Perth Amboy; it was unexpectedly modest, as was the salary that went with it.

With William and Elizabeth settled in Perth Amboy, Franklin and Debbie discussed their own plans for a house in Philadelphia. It would be built on a plot of land made up of bits and pieces purchased from relatives, and clustered around the edges of a larger plot that was Debbie's inheritance—all of it only yards from the place on Market Street where she first caught sight of her future husband. It would be spacious, although not grand (Franklin was opposed on principle to grandeur); it would have comfortable rooms for guests, with one room set aside for the glass armonica, Sally's harpsichord, and Franklin's electrical equipment. At some stage of their planning it was decided that this music room would be blue, and Debbie, whose spelling was uncertain, thought of it as the Blewroom.

Would she go back with him to England? He knew she would not—yet he had been longing to return even before leaving London. Now, as winter turned to spring and carpenters working on the house were followed by plasterers, it seemed increasingly likely that he would get his wish.

Several years had passed since Franklin and William attended the Albany Congress and parleyed with Iroquois leaders; the French and Indian War had ended with an English victory, and the French were essentially pushed out of the North American mainland. But for the Indians nothing was changed. Europeans were still gobbling up their land, and would continue to do so whether they were French, English, or Spanish. Frontier forts, from the Great Lakes to the Gulf of Mexico, were under constant attack by Indians, and colonists responded by raiding Indian settlements—indiscriminately, as if all Indians were interchangeable, and loyal, longtime friends could be held responsible for the deeds of combat-loving militants. This was how it happened that in December of 1764, in the little Pennsylvania town of Lancaster, fourteen members of the peaceable Conestoga tribe were set upon and slaughtered in their sleep by a mob from the nearby town of Paxton.

Three months later several hundred settlers joined the "Paxton Boys" as they marched on Philadelphia, demanding surrender of some 140 Indians under the protection of Quakers and other pacifists. As the mob neared the city, the new Governor—who else but young John Penn—turned for help to Franklin, one of his commissioners of defense.

It must have been a sweet moment for Franklin, and he made good use of it. Within three days he had put together a militia, and with a deputation of citizens came face-to-face with the mob, heard them out, persuaded them that the city was prepared to defend itself—even some Quakers were armed, he said—and reached an agreement: "The fighting face we put on and the reasonings we used . . . turned them back and restored quiet to the city."

But it wasn't finished for Franklin. The blood of the murdered Conestogas cried out for justice, yet Governor Penn had no interest in justice for Indians. The Assembly passed a militia bill and a money bill, and Penn vetoed both, then offered bounties for Indian scalps, whether men's or women's. Even the scalps of children were welcome, although they earned no bounty.

"I don't love the Proprietary [Penn], and . . . he does not love me," Franklin said. "Our totally different Tempers forbid it." Once again he called for the colony to be taken from the Proprietors and put into royal hands.

The Governor's party, already campaigning for October elections, concentrated on Franklin's extravagance in London, his immorality in general, and the electrical discoveries they claimed were mostly stolen from others. Franklin lost the election by twenty-five votes (out of four thousand) thus losing his seat in the Assembly after fourteen years. Nevertheless, his party had won a majority in Pennsylvania, and its members were determined to send him back to England with a petition to the King.

He left in November 1764, while some three hundred supporters cheered him on, firing cannons and singing a song that called on God to save King George and Benjamin Franklin.

Chapter Eleven

Questions

Almost his last thought before sailing
was of his daughter, Sally. In a letter
written from an island in the Delaware River

before the ship took off, he reminded her that he had enemies:

> and very bitter ones, and you must expect their Enmity will ex-
> tend in some degree to you, so that your slightest Indiscretions
> will be magnified into crimes, in order the more sensibly to
> wound and afflict me.
>
> Go constantly to Church whoever preaches . . . I am the
> more particular on this Head, as you seemed to express a little
> before I came away some Inclination to leave our Church,
> which I would not have you do.

She must never miss a prayer day, he said, nor "despise Sermons
even of the Preachers you dislike, for the Discourse is often much
better than the Man, as sweet and clear Waters come to us through
very dirty earth."

Sally was nineteen, old enough to have her own opinions and
to resent her father's instructing her to do what he didn't, namely,
go constantly to church. As for Debbie, she, too, was left behind,
but she had the house to care for—heating stoves to install, rooms
to be painted, although the painting of the Blewroom would have
to wait until her husband's return. Whatever she did for the house
was proof that he would come back to it, and her letters were full of
domestic detail, warmhearted and loving, sometimes confused, always unmistakably hers.

"Dear child," she began one letter—he usually started the same way—"O my dear hough hapey am I to hear that you air safe and well. Hough dus your armes doe . . . o I long to know." The marble fireplace had come, and she had bought one more piece of land adjoining theirs, this time a good-sized one. After more news about the house and relatives, the letter ended as it always did: "your a feck shonet wife." Her phonetic spelling was not unusual for women of her generation.

But by the spring of 1765 Debbie's letters were more concerned with politics than housekeeping. Philadelphia, like the rest of America, was hopping mad about a proposed Stamp Act. Prestamped and official papers were to be used for all legal transactions; there were forty-three such uses, including wills, marriage licenses, and the wrappings of playing cards. The money raised in this way would help pay for English troops quartered in the colonies as protection against Indian raids; it would also whittle down the considerable debt left by the French and Indian War.

To Franklin, the Stamp Act was a minor matter, and he had trouble understanding why people were so worked up about it. Mobs took to the streets in Boston and attacked the homes of government officials. Crude figures of these same officials were hanged from tree branches. In Philadelphia, there were accusations that Franklin had helped frame the Stamp Act, that he was plotting to become the next Governor of Pennsylvania. William divided his time between Perth Amboy and Philadelphia, defending his father on all sides.

In mid-September, rumors spread through town about an angry

mob making ready to march on Franklin's house. William implored his mother and sister once and for all to come home with him; Sally agreed, but Debbie refused to leave her new house. When her cousin Josiah Davenport offered to stay with her, she told him to bring a gun. No, two guns. Her brother brought another, and together they turned one of the upstairs rooms into a storehouse for weapons and ammunition. Then Debbie boarded up the house and prepared to defy the first stranger who crossed her doorstep. She had done nothing wrong, she said, her husband had done nothing wrong, and she would not be made uneasy by anybody, nor would she stir or show the least anxiety. As it happened, Joseph Galloway, an assemblyman and longtime friend of Franklin's, rounded up several hundred supporters to police the streets on the night of the projected attack, and the angry mob retreated, then disappeared.

When Franklin heard about it two months later, he told Debbie, "I honour much the Spirit and Courage you showed and the prudent Preparations you made in that Time of Danger. The Woman deserves a good house that is determined to defend it."

In London the Stamp Act passed both houses of Parliament. Regrettable, Franklin said, but it couldn't be helped: "We might as well have hindered the sun's setting." Many Americans were less philosophical. There was stubborn resistance, often well organized, and widespread refusal to buy any English goods until the "cruel act" was repealed.

Franklin began to see that this Stamp Act could be enforced only with bayonets. He launched a publicity campaign, starting with a cartoon of his own design that showed Great Britain as a beggar, her severed limbs scattered around her, the limbs labeled New York, Virginia, Pennsylvania, New England—this was what would happen to the Mother Country if she persisted in pushing her children so hard they broke off relations. He used the cartoon as his letterhead, while churning out articles for British newspapers under a variety of pen names—Pacificus, Homespun, The Traveler.

In a letter to the *Public Advertiser* he told readers that the British wool industry had no chance against the American, because "the very Tails of the American Sheep are so laden with Wool, that each has a Car or Waggon on four little Wheels, to support and keep it from trailing on the Ground." By the beginning of 1766 business organizations all over England were petitioning the government for repeal of the Stamp Act. And in mid-February, Franklin was one of thirty Americans summoned before Parliament to explain why their countrymen were so stubbornly resisting.

As the British statesman Edmund Burke described it, seeing Franklin questioned in Parliament was like watching a schoolmaster being quizzed by a herd of schoolboys. He answered two hours' worth of questions with his usual wit and common sense: If the Stamp Act were made less burdensome, would Americans submit to it? "No, never, unless compelled by force of arms." And what was American opinion about Britain before 1763? "The best in the world . . . Numerous as the people are in the several old provinces, they cost you nothing in forts, citadels, garrisons or armies, to keep them in subjection. They were governed by this country at the expence only of a little pen, ink and paper. They were led by a thread. They had not only a respect, but an affection for Great Britain."

Within a very few weeks the act was repealed—largely because of demands from mercantile interests in Britain, who had seen their businesses disintegrate before their eyes, but the well-reasoned argument of Dr. Franklin was also a factor. Shipping started up again—teapots, tea, ribbons, carpets, and slippers appeared once more in American shops. The empire Franklin loved and believed in—he compared it to a fine and noble China vase—had held together.

There was unpleasant news from home now; ignoring her father's wishes and advice, Sally had married Richard Bache, a businessman, although not a prosperous one. Franklin had all but forbidden the match—let the young man succeed before undertaking the support of a wife, he said—but after a very long engagement he was simply overruled.

With Sally's wedding behind her, Debbie begged to know when Franklin was coming home. He said he would be back next winter. Possibly next spring. A letter to William spoke of his return in a matter of weeks, unless he were offered some government post more profitable than the deputy postmastership. Government posts and titles seemed always to hover in the background of Franklin's London years—as possible bribes, or else rewards that somehow never came to pass.

And now another marriage was on the horizon. While on a seaside holiday with her aunt, Polly Stevenson had "met with a very sensible Physician . . . I would not have you or my Mother sur-

THE EMPIRE FRANKLIN LOVED AND BELIEVED IN ... HAD HELD TOGETHER.

prised," she wrote Franklin, "if I should run off with this young man; to be sure it would be an imprudent Step at the discreet Age of Thirty." The "Physician" was William Hewson, a surgeon and distinguished anatomist who later became a member of the Royal Society and was honored with their Copley Medal. Not even Franklin could doubt that this gifted young man deserved his "dear good Girl," and when the two were married the following summer, it was Franklin who gave the bride away.

A few months later, when Mrs. Stevenson left for a short holiday, Dr. Hewson and Polly came to Craven Street to keep Franklin company, and the three of them put out a satirical newspaper, the *Cravenstreet Gazette*, modeled after the court calendar: "We hear that the *great* Person (so called from his enormous Size) of a certain Family in a certain Street, is grievously affected at the late Changes [Mrs. Stevenson's departure], and could hardly be comforted this Morning, though the new Ministry promised him a roasted Shoulder of Mutton, and Potatoes, for his Dinner."

Within the year Polly produced a baby boy, christened William, with Franklin for his godfather, and that was the end of her interest in science. But if Franklin had lost a pupil, he had gained an attentive and devoted second family, complete with an infant to hold on his knee.

A letter from Debbie wanted instructions about the Blewroom; when he replied, her husband asked for the dimensions of certain windows in order to buy curtain fabric that he would bring when he returned. Soon, he said. Or next spring. He named several different times.

About the Assembly's petition asking that Pennsylvania be taken out of the Penns' hands, eleven months had now gone by without an answer. At the end of that time, Franklin was told the petition could not be put before the King. The next step would be resubmitting it, which might well take another eleven months, if not more. One result of Franklin's testimony before Parliament regarding the Stamp Act was that political conservatives—Tories—now saw him as a potential traitor, certainly a dangerous man.

When Lord Charles Townshend, newly appointed as Chancellor of the Exchequer (Secretary of the Treasury), decided to tax a number of imported goods entering America—paper, paint, tea, and lead among them—Franklin urged Americans to be sensible about the new taxes (which came to be called the Townshend duties). Parliament flatters itself, he said, "that you cannot long subsist without their Manufactures—they imagine the Colonies will differ among themselves, deceive and desert one another, and quietly one after the other submit to the Yoke and return to the use of British Fineries." Don't do it, he said. Be thrifty, go without, or else make it yourself.

William pointed out that England stood to lose far more through American boycotts than she could possibly gain from taxes. He and his father were in agreement about English politics at this point, both of them deploring the King's Tory ministers and their conservative policies. Several political figures were friends of Franklin's, but like Edmund Burke they were Whigs—liberals and intellectuals—and for the present they were not in power.

Franklin wrote to a Boston friend, Samuel Cooper, "Let us . . . hold fast our loyalty to our King . . . as that steady loyalty is the most probable means of securing us from the arbitrary power of a corrupt Parliament that does not like us and conceives itself to have an interest in keeping us down and fleecing us." His affection for the King never wavered, not yet. "I wish to see a steady dutiful attachment to the King and his family maintained among us," he wrote to Thomas Cushing, a Massachusetts politician.

In the winter of 1768–69, Franklin had a letter from Thomas Bond, a longtime friend who was the family physician, saying Debbie had suffered a stroke that left her "with a partial Palsy in the Tongue, and a sudden Loss of Memory, which alarmed us much, but she soon recovered from them, though her constitution in general appears impaired. These are bad Symptoms in advanced Life and Augur Danger of further Injury on the Nervous System." But when Debbie was able to write for herself, she told her "dear child" that her severest symptom was not physical pain but rather a "dissatisfied distress," by which she meant the years of waiting for her husband to come home to her.

Franklin's sister Jane left Boston to care for Debbie, but it was Sally who provided the best of all remedies by giving birth to her first child, a boy she named Benjamin Franklin Bache. Debbie called him her Kingbird.

Franklin did nothing to relieve his wife's distress; he was comfortable, happy, and busy where he was. No longer the agent only for Pennsylvania, he also represented Georgia, New Jersey, and

Massachusetts, and had become in effect America's representative in London. An extensive correspondence on scientific subjects kept him in touch with friends and acquaintances in England, America, and France. To William Brownrigg, a physician and active researcher, Franklin wrote a letter long and detailed enough to stand on its own as a paper in a scholarly journal. The subject was how oil smoothed troubled waters.

Whenever he went into the countryside, Franklin said, "I contrived to take with me . . . a little Oil in the upper hollow joint of my bamboo Cane" so as to be ready to spread it on water when "an Opportunity should offer":

> In these Experiments, one Circumstance struck me with particular Surprize. This was the sudden, wide and forcible Spreading of a Drop of Oil on the Face of the Water, which I do not know that any body has hitherto considered. If a Drop of Oil is put on a polished Marble Table, or on a Looking Glass that lies horizontally, the Drop remains in its Place, spreading very little. But when put on Water it spreads instantly many feet round, becoming [extremely thin, and eventually] so much thinner as to be invisible except in its Effect of Smoothing the Waves at a much greater Distance.

What was the reason for it? Why did a drop of oil put on a mirror remain in place, while the same drop of oil if put on water in a pond spread itself instantly very thin? At a guess, he supposed the following:

It seems as if a mutual Repulsion between its Particles took Place as soon as it touched the Water, and a Repulsion so strong as to act on other Bodies swimming on the Surface, as Straws, Leaves, Chips, &c. forcing them to recede every way from the Drop, as from a Center, leaving a large clear Space. The Quantity of this Force, and the Distance to which it will operate, I have not yet ascertained, but I think it a curious Enquiry, and I wish to understand whence it arises.

So there was a good deal to keep him occupied. It was about this time, for example, that Temple, William's son, began appearing in the Stevenson household. Away at school most of the year, he was now about fourteen and old enough to join his grandfather during vacations. When Mrs. Stevenson and Polly saw the resemblance between the two, they understood this was not the child of some distant relation.

Chapter Twelve

Franklin under Siege

Wearing a full-bottomed wig and a suit of brown Manchester velvet he was especially proud of, Franklin stood to one side of the great fireplace, facing a large bow window. A long table ran below it, and around the table sat thirty-six members of the Privy Council, among them nine peers of the realm; Lord North, the Prime Minister; and the Archbishop of Canterbury.

This room was called the Cockpit. Years earlier, it had been the site of an actual cockpit, where fighting roosters battled to the death while their owners bet on the outcome. Now it was part of a jumble of government offices known as Whitehall, and used for meetings of the Prime Minister and the Privy Council. Today, January 29, 1774, the room was packed, mostly with men and women of the upper nobility. There was an air of eager anticipation, as if the audience had been promised a spectacle. Yet there would be no battle to the death today, no sharpened claws, no blood-spattered handlers. Strictly speaking, no actual blood would be shed.

To understand the significance of the day's events, it is necessary to go back several years to March of 1770, when two British regiments were stationed at the Boston waterfront. It was a troubled, often riotous place and the townspeople hated the sight of the soldiers. One day at the end of a long winter, a small mob advanced on the British barracks, shouting obscenities, pitching rocks, chunks of ice, and oyster shells at the soldiers. Some soldiers fired back, killing five of the townspeople and wounding several others. Americans called it the Boston Massacre.

Franklin didn't blame the soldiers; neither did William, or the Virginia planter George Washington. John Adams, a Massachusetts lawyer, maintained that the redcoats had fired in self-defense. But

King George III agreed to remove the two regiments, and the Townshend duties were repealed—except for tea.

To avoid paying the tea tax, American merchants smuggled in tea from Holland—and the British East India Company, formerly the chief supplier of tea to the colonies, suffered financially. Its leaders asked Parliament for help, and Parliament responded by permitting the company to sell its tea below the price of smuggled tea. In Philadelphia and New York, crowds of angry citizens began roaming the waterfront, refusing to let the British tea ships dock and unload. And in December of 1773, the radicals of Boston, led by a band of activists—artisans and shopkeepers calling themselves the Sons of Liberty—put on the war paint of Mohawk braves and boarded three tea ships. With "an hideous yelling," they emptied 342 chests of tea into the sea. It was a very great deal of tea, and it was worth (at one estimate) about a million dollars in today's money.

This news reached England, and Franklin, on January 20, 1774. The date is significant because the event at the Cockpit, the one that attracted such a crowd of wellborn spectators, had been scheduled for January 29. The arrangement had been made months earlier, well before news of the Boston Tea Party arrived in London, and its purpose was entirely independent of Boston, as we will see. But the news from Boston greatly increased the British government's opposition to Americans in general, and to Franklin in particular.

Franklin thoroughly disapproved of the tea dumping, called it an "act of violent injustice on our part," and even offered to pay for

the tea out of his own pocket, provided the acts against Massachusetts were repealed—a condition that made his offer impossible to
accept. But Franklin's ideas about Mother England and the colonies
were changing. It had been nearly four years since he became the
agent—the spokesman—for Massachusetts, the most radical of the
thirteen colonies. Protesters in Boston claimed the right to govern
and tax themselves, denying Parliament any authority over them.
Even the Crown, they said, did not deserve their loyalty or obedi-
ence.

There were times now when Franklin sounded like a Boston
radical himself. "Parliament has no right to make any laws whatever
binding on the colonies," he wrote to his son, the Royal Governor
of New Jersey. But as deputy postmaster-general, Franklin was also a
servant of the Crown. And he believed, he had always believed, in
a great English-speaking commonwealth through which England
and America would one day rule the world—while the King, in
partnership with the colonial Assemblies, would rule the colonies.
Little wonder that he was accused "in England of being too much
an American, and in America of being too much an Englishman."
And while his English and American halves carried on their internal debate, the gathering storm prepared to break over Franklin's
head.

It started with six letters written in 1772 by the Massachusetts
Governor, Thomas Hutchinson, and addressed to an English official; their subject was the rebellious behavior of the colonists. To
control them, Hutchinson said, the British government would be

AND WHILE
HIS ENGLISH
AND

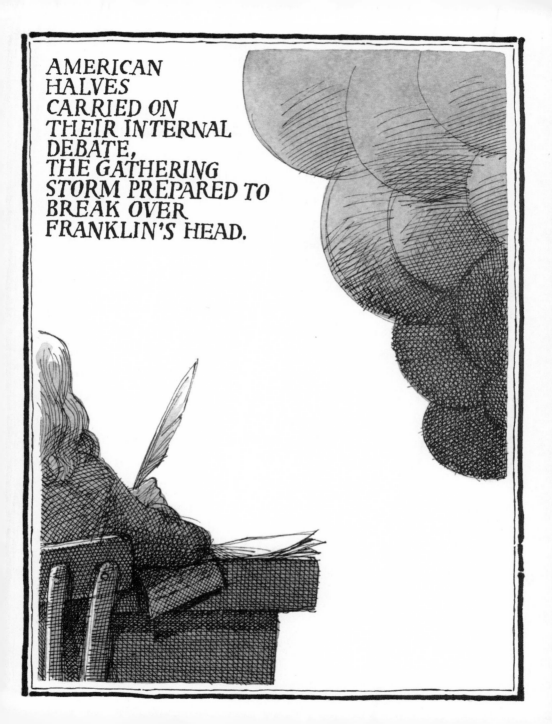

well advised to take stronger measures, even including "an abridge-ment of what are called English liberties."

One way or another—no one has ever learned how—Hutchin-son's letters fell into Franklin's hands. He sent them back to Massa-chusetts, to the Speaker of that colony's House of Representatives, with many words of caution—no one was to know that he, Franklin, had sent the letters, and the contents must be kept secret. They were not, of course, kept secret and in 1773 even appeared in the *Boston Gazette*.

Franklin finally confessed that he was the one who got hold of the letters and released them to the world. How did he get them? From whom did he get them? And what did he think the letters proved? He never answered the first two questions. About the third he said, "Their tendency was to incense the Mother Country against her colonies," then to widen the breach between them. From start to finish, the business of the Hutchinson letters was tan-gled, mysterious, and ill fated. And from start to finish, Franklin was less than candid about it.

In early December, the British ministry began to consider a petition from the Massachusetts Assembly to remove Hutchinson from office. Two things happened as a result: Hutchinson hired a lawyer to represent him, and Franklin was ordered to appear at a hearing related to the petition. This was the event scheduled to take place on January 29, 1774, in the Cockpit before the Privy Council and the audience of hostile upper-level peers.

They, the upper nobility, had been cool to Franklin all along;

even before the happenings in Boston, they had seen him as a representative of the colonial mob. Unattractive to begin with, that mob had grown increasingly disloyal. Now, at last, they would have the pleasure of seeing Franklin tormented (he said later the hearing was like a "bull baiting") by the lawyer Hutchinson chose to represent him, Alexander Wedderburn, the King's solicitor-general.

Wedderburn was a man said to be ferocious in attack, whose vocabulary came from the gutter. At least one historian claims that Wedderburn's language at the Cockpit was so foul that London newspapers avoided a full account of the proceedings. His tactic was to demolish Franklin's character by insisting he had stolen personal letters—although the six letters were hardly personal, being concerned solely with public affairs, and would have had no value otherwise—and that his motive for such crude behavior was to disgrace Hutchinson and become Governor of Massachusetts himself.

Franklin was a common thief, fraudulent and corrupt, Wedderburn said, and then went on: "I hope, my Lords, you will mark and brand that man, for the honour of this country, of Europe, and of Mankind . . . He has forfeited all the respect of societies and of men. Into what companies will he hereafter go with an unembarrassed face?" Men would watch him with a jealous eye, they would hide their papers from him and lock up their desks.

Wedderburn's tirade continued for close to an hour, with Franklin standing silent, almost motionless, in his old-fashioned wig and velvet suit. He had just passed his sixty-eighth birthday, but he gave no sign of weariness, and several observers remarked that his expression never once changed. He had composed his face into a mask of wooden serenity, and he kept it serene until the end.

For most of the audience, Wedderburn's performance was a delight. In Franklin's words, "They seemed to enjoy highly the entertainment, and frequently broke out in loud applauses." Two days later he was stripped of his postmastership.

Humiliated, without influence, aware that there were men in high places working to see him imprisoned, Franklin knew that London papers were calling him "Old Doubleface," and "this old snake," and "the living emblem of iniquity in grey hairs." But his public face remained expressionless. His suffering was done in private, perhaps concealed even from himself; he wrote to his sister Jane, "They are every now and then reporting here, that I am using Means to get again into Office. Perhaps they wish I would. But they may expect it till Doomsday. For God knows my Heart, I would not accept the best Office the King has to bestow."

To the Dutch physician Jan Ingenhousz, the discoverer of photosynthesis and now court physician in Vienna, he wrote: "I do not find that I have lost a single friend on the Occasion. All have visited me repeatedly with affectionate Assurances of their unalterable Respect and Affection." This was not the whole truth; several long-time friends were very much distressed by Franklin's silence about how he got the letters. David Hume, historian and philosopher, believed that Wedderburn's treatment of Franklin was cruel but not unjustified; according to Sir John Pringle, if Franklin had asked for advice, anyone with tact and common sense would have persuaded him not to make such use of private correspondence.

When rejecting the petition that called for Governor Hutchinson's removal, the Privy Council suggested there was something traitorous about the very act of submitting such a petition—as if Americans had lost the right to complain and were second-class citizens now. Yet Franklin didn't go home. His effectiveness as the London spokesman for the colonies had evaporated overnight, but he stayed on at Craven Street, and was there when another blow fell.

He wrote to Debbie three months after the ordeal at the Cockpit: "Our Family here is in great Distress. Poor Mrs. Hewson has lost her husband. He died . . . of a Fever which baffled the Skill of our best Physicians. He was an excellent young Man, ingenious, industrious, useful, and beloved by all that knew him. She is left with two young Children, and a third soon expected . . . They were a happy Couple! All their Schemes of Life are now overthrown!"

Two days later he wrote to Debbie again: "It is now a very long time indeed since I have had the Pleasure of a Line from you."

A letter from William, written on Christmas Eve, began: "Honoured Father, I came here on Thursday last to attend the Funeral of my poor old Mother . . . I heartily wish you had happened to have come over in the Fall, as I think her disappointment in that respect preyed a good deal on her spirits." As before, he urged his father to come home, and told him to bring Temple with him when he did. After thirteen childless years, William and his wife had come to accept that Temple was the only family they would ever have.

There were legal matters to attend to in Philadelphia that had been left in Debbie's hands—yet another reason to return. About

Debbie herself, and the loss of his wife after more than forty years, Franklin said nothing, ever, or at least nothing that leaves any trace. And even while he considered the need to leave, and mulled over the choices of when to leave, he had half a mind to return to Craven Street in the fall.

During the first months of 1775—the last months of his time in England—he was approached by several people in positions of importance who were trying to head off what they saw as a looming disaster for both sides. One was William Pitt; as Prime Minister during the Seven Years' War, Pitt had led England to victory against France. Now he was Lord Chatham, and determined to put before the House of Lords a workable plan for reconciliation between Great Britain and her colonies. To form such a plan, Chatham believed he needed the cooperation of Franklin, whom he had essentially ignored until now. Swallowing his pride, he paid a call to Craven Street—a visit that "flattered not a little my vanity," Franklin said, "and gave me the more pleasure as it happened on the very day twelvemonth that the Ministry had taken so many pains to disgrace me before the Privy Council."

Chatham "mentioned an Opinion prevailing here that America aimed at setting up for herself as an independent State . . . I assured him, that having more than once traveled almost from one end of the Continent to the other and kept a great variety of Company, eating, drinking and conversing with them freely, I never had heard in any Conversation from any Person drunk or sober, the least Expression of a Wish for a Separation."

The reconciliation plan Chatham and Franklin worked out together was presented to the Lords early in 1775—and then buried, totally, finally. So were other plans created with other influential acquaintances, or even comparative strangers who approached Franklin because they were suddenly overtaken by fear of a long, costly, and brutal war between brothers. Franklin threw himself into each of these attempts, which always failed, and to see them "so ignominiously rejected by so great a Majority, and so hastily too . . . made [Parliament's] Claim of Sovereignty over three Millions of virtuous sensible People in America, seem the greatest of Absurdities, since they appeared to have scarce Discretion enough to govern a Herd of Swine."

His last day in London, in March of 1775, was spent with the chemist Joseph Priestley, looking through the American newspapers together, with Franklin choosing passages for his English friend to offer to the press. A war was inevitable, he said, stopping for a moment because his eyes filled with tears. America would surely win that war, he went on, but it would take ten years and he would not live to see the end of it, tears now streaming down his face.

The next day Franklin and his grandson set off for the harbor town of Portsmouth and the Pennsylvania packet. While at sea Temple helped with the daily task of gathering data for his grandfather's ongoing study of the Gulf Stream—six years earlier Franklin had learned about its existence from a cousin, Timothy Folger, a whaling captain. Now a thermometer filled with mercury and alcohol was lowered over the ship's side and into the ocean five times a day. Within the stream, they found an abundance of gulfweed, and warmer temperatures than in the sea on either side of it. Franklin also noticed that the Gulf Stream "does not sparkle in the night."

When he wasn't above deck with Temple, he was at work in the cabin, composing an account of the secret negotiations that occupied his last months in London. Ninety-six pages long, it took the form of a letter to William, intended to show him the stubbornness and stupidity of the British government.

While Franklin was still at sea, British soldiers clashed with American patriots at Lexington, Massachusetts, and at nearby Concord. An undeclared and unofficial sort of war had begun; when Franklin came ashore in May of 1775, he was immediately pulled into it.

Chapter Thirteen

To France
on a Secret Mission

December 3, 1776: a fishing vessel
makes its way toward a small
village, Auray, on the coast
of Brittany in northwestern France.

There are three passengers, Benjamin Franklin and his grandsons—
Temple, almost seventeen, and seven-year-old Benjamin Franklin
Bache—Benny, the Kingbird.

Aboard the American ship *Reprisal*, they have endured a miserable midwinter crossing. There was a real possibility of capture by
the British, in which case Franklin could have been hanged as a
traitor. But at the moment what he fears most is nausea—the voyage has "almost demolished" him, he says. For the past few days the
Reprisal has lain at anchor in Quiberon Bay, awaiting a lull in the
storm so she can proceed to Nantes; from Nantes, Franklin had
planned to travel overland to Paris. But he's not sure he can survive
another hour aboard ship, and the captain has hailed this fishing
boat to put his feet on land as soon as possible.

Unable to stand when they come ashore, Franklin has to be
carried to the inn. At the age of seventy, he suffers from a mixed
bag of ailments, one of which is gout, a painful affliction of the legs
and feet. A troublesome rash on his head—he calls it "scurf"—has
begun spreading "to all the small of my back, on my sides, my legs
and my arms, besides what continued under my hair." To keep his
head warm while at the same time concealing the scurf, he has
taken to wearing a cap made of marten fur.

Eighteen eventful months have passed between his leaving
England and setting out for France. The day after his arrival in
Philadelphia, Franklin was named by the Pennsylvania Assembly as
a delegate to the second Continental Congress. The first, in the autumn of 1774, had advised the colonies to begin training citizens for

UNABLE TO STAND WHEN THEY COME ASHORE, FRANKLIN HAS TO BE CARRIED TO THE INN.

war, although nobody at that first Congress wanted war, and nobody
mentioned independence. Like Franklin, what they wanted was for
Parliament to restore their English liberties.

In spite of his age, at this second Congress Franklin became a
workhorse, serving at one time or another on thirty-four committees. One was charged with writing a Declaration of Independence.
Another, the Committee of Secret Correspondence, would take up
relations with foreign countries (later, it became the State Department). A month after George Washington's appointment as commander in chief of a continental army, Franklin became the young
nation's first postmaster-general; he directed that his salary be used
for the benefit of wounded soldiers.

He had been living with Sally and her family in the new house
on Market Street, while Temple was in New Jersey visiting the father he had hardly ever seen—and longed to know. The two elder
Franklins, Benjamin and William, patriot and loyalist, had been
moving apart. Their meetings were increasingly painful, and usually
turned into shouting matches—because William kept faith with
England and the King, as well as the oaths he had sworn as Royal
Governor in Perth Amboy while his father had stood by, happy for
him and proud of him.

Now Franklin had had his fill of Mother England and the
King—he would have spit them out if he could. He no longer
wanted Governor William Franklin to visit him in Philadelphia,
saying the presence of this loyalist son embarrassed him. He wrote
to his old friend in England William Strahan: "You are a Member

of Parliament, and one of that Majority which has doomed my Country to Destruction. You have begun to burn our Towns, and murder our People. Look upon your Hands! They are stained with the Blood of your Relations! You and I were long Friends. You are now my Enemy, and I am, Yours, B. Franklin." The letter was never mailed.

That winter a foreign agent had appeared in Philadelphia, a young Frenchman by the name of Achard de Bonvouloir. He went to a bookshop that specialized in French publications and asked if the bookseller happened to know a certain Benjamin Franklin.

Yes, yes, the man said, everyone in Philadelphia knew him. Why was the gentleman inquiring?

Because I would like very much to meet him, Bonvouloir said.

The bookseller spoke to Franklin, who agreed, and there were several meetings, all secret; at first it was only the two of them, then there were four more, the members of the Committee of Secret Correspondence. "Each comes by dusk by different routes to a marked place," Bonvouloir said when writing home. The marked place was the Philadelphia Carpenters' Hall, and the meetings proceeded slowly because neither side knew how far the other was authorized to go.

Suppose there should be an absolute break between England and America, followed by full-scale war. In that case the Americans already knew they could face England only in alliance with a powerful partner, one who would furnish ammunition and weapons, preferably on credit. The Committee of Secret Correspondence had exactly that purpose in mind, and France was the first nation they had planned to approach.

As for the French, they were eager to strike a body blow at England, their ancient enemy. But they could not risk a formal alliance with a nation incapable of facing England—a nation likely to be defeated by England. Furthermore, the Americans had not declared their independence, which brought up another difficulty: so long as they were colonies rebelling against British rule, the French were not free to trade with them, since Britain would take it as a cause for war, and France could not afford another war; the French treasury still suffered from the last one. But once America declared independence, trade would be possible—the New World had tobacco, cotton, rice, indigo, and a fortune in furs.

In Carpenters' Hall the committee all but promised to declare independence; there would be no going back, they said, and Bonvouloir was impressed. At the end of December he submitted a favorable report to the man who had sent him to America, the French foreign minister, Charles Gravier, Count de Vergennes.

At more or less the same time George Washington wrote to the Congress, "Our want of Powder [gunpowder] is inconceivable." At a later date, "Our situation in the Article of Powder is much more alarming than I had the most distant Idea of." Franklin suggested pikes—long wooden spears—but even before he offered that suggestion, Washington had ordered four dozen spears, "thirteen feet in length, and the wood part a good deal more substantial than those already made." Writing to one of Washington's generals,

Franklin said, "I still wish, with you, that Pikes could be introduced, and I would add Bows and Arrows. These were good Weapons, not wisely laid aside."

Meanwhile, backstage and well under cover, a French company was being created for the purpose of shipping wine and delicacies to the West Indies. The company, the wine, and the delicacies were an illusion, but the ships were real. Their cargo would include 58 brass cannons, 110 barrels of excellent gunpowder, and tents sufficient for ten thousand, as well as shoes, stockings, blankets, carriages, and gunworms, the screws used to withdraw charges from muzzle-loaded firearms. To deliver this cargo, the ships would have to mark time in the Indies, while awaiting an opportunity to run the British blockade of American coasts; it was not until March of 1777 that the first French supply ships would reach ports in New Hampshire.

Franklin hoped to persuade the French to lend, sell, or give everything else—money, troops, fighting ships. Great Britain's navy was the most powerful in the Western world, while the Americans had no ships, just as they had no arms industry and no army. Militia was what they had, volunteer citizen soldiers. Washington believed he could build a professional army, one that would carry modern weapons and ammunition, and face the British as equals.

The Declaration of Independence was composed largely by Thomas Jefferson with little help from Franklin, who suggested only a few changes of phrase—but Franklin stood solidly behind its principles. And when the Continental Congress realized the Americans needed a representative in Paris, he was the obvious choice. Years later John Adams explained this decision: "Who, in the name of astonishment, in all America, at that time had a knowledge of courts? Franklin alone had resided in England . . . at the Court of St. James. In address and good breeding, he was excelled by very few." He went as part of a three-man commission, the others being Silas Deane, a Connecticut congressman, and Arthur Lee, a lawyer then living in England. Both were in their early forties and had no experience with courts or diplomacy.

Before leaving for France, Franklin withdrew between three and four thousand pounds from the bank and lent it to the Congress along with all the money he could raise. Too old and ailing for such a voyage, he was nevertheless determined to go, and to take Temple with him.

The boy was in Perth Amboy at the time, with his stepmother—his father having been clapped into prison in Connecticut as a "virulent enemy to this country, and a person that may prove dangerous." Temple set his heart on a visit to his father; for his stepmother, too, the chance to contact her husband, to put in his hands a letter carried by this devoted son, offered some crumbs of comfort in her loneliness. Temple, the good grandson, asked his grandfather's permission to undertake the journey—

Franklin told him no; his tone was brusque. Soon Temple learned that something entirely different was in progress; instead of continuing his education in the fall, he would be sailing to France with his grandfather. William knew nothing about it. Apparently

Franklin never asked his permission to take this only child abroad, and William first found out when the business was well under way. He managed to console himself with the belief that "the old gentleman" would enroll the boy in some foreign university. Certainly this was part of Franklin's reason for taking him to France, that Temple would complete his education there, or else gain enough experience in diplomacy to build a career. Another reason was that Temple bore the Franklin name, and even looked like his grandfather. But all these reasonings were only pieces of the whole truth, which was simpler: Franklin loved the boy, intensely and unwisely.

Franklin's reasons for bringing his other grandson, Benny Bache, the Kingbird, are less clear—shy and withdrawn, he enjoyed tagging after Temple but was painfully in awe of his grandfather.

When the three of them set off aboard the *Reprisal* with their every move noted by the all-seeing eyes of British intelligence, the Marquis of Rockingham had this to say about Franklin's midwinter voyage: "I cannot refrain from paying my tribute of admiration to the vigour, magnanimity, and determined resolution of the Old Man."

Lord Stormont, Britain's ambassador to France, took a different view of Franklin: "I look upon him as a dangerous Engine."

Chapter Fourteen

Astonishing News from Saratoga

The day after he reached Paris, Franklin composed a note to Vergennes, the French foreign minister. He said the three commissioners—himself, Silas Deane, and Arthur Lee—were empowered by the Continental Congress "to propose and negotiate a treaty of amity and commerce between France and the United States." Temple carried the note to Vergennes.

Five days later, Franklin, Deane, and Lee (along with a young American, Dr. Edward Bancroft, acting as temporary secretary) were received by the Count de Vergennes. A career diplomat and passionate patriot, he longed to see England laid low, and if the instrument of England's downfall should be a colonial rebellion—intended to replace an anointed king with a republican apparatus—that was a pity, but one had to use the tools that came to hand.

Reporting to the Congress about this first interview, the commissioners said they had been met with the greatest courtesy but that no real negotiations were possible, according to Vergennes—no "open reception and acknowledgment of us," because of the treaties with England. Of course the ports of France were open to American shipping, and as friends they were most welcome to buy or sell, to import, export—

And all this time, the account continues, not one word was spoken by the foreign minister about the cannons, fieldpieces, and gunpowder that had been taken out of royal storehouses for shipment to America. Vergennes knew it just as the commissioners knew it, but not a word, not even a whisper. Spies were everywhere. As it happened, the very personable Dr. Bancroft was discovered, years later, to have been a British spy. Using invisible ink, he wrote a dispatch once each week, sealed it in a bottle, and put the bottle in a hole in a tree in one of the city's public gardens. There it waited to be picked up at half-past nine on Tuesdays, by someone from the British embassy.

What Franklin did next was move out of his Left Bank hotel to a small village, Passy, about a mile from the city. There he and his grandsons settled into one wing of a mansion that belonged to Jacques de Chaumont. A wealthy and ambitious businessman, Chaumont was involved in the supply of arms to America, and hoped for a variety of commercial contracts in the future. According to his competitors, "He would grasp, if he could, the commerce of the thirteen colonies for himself alone."

Chaumont might have been persuaded by Vergennes to get Franklin away from the center of Paris, where all his comings and goings were public; on this country estate it was thought that Franklin had some protection from spies. Silas Deane lived there for a time, as did Edward Bancroft; Arthur Lee, the third commissioner, was invited to live at the Chaumont home but preferred not to.

Nothing in Franklin's experience had prepared him for the scale and splendor of the place, the parks and gardens, the courtyards, the terrace overlooking the river and the distant spires of Paris—or the corps of liveried servants, nine for his household alone, who bowed deeply, opened doors for him and his grandsons, and never smiled. With the Chaumont family, Franklin charmed the women as he had once charmed Mrs. Stevenson and Polly. Here there were three daughters, and in his wobbly French, Franklin adopted all three; to their great delight they became "my child," "my wife," and "my dear friend." When he began to entertain, it was Madame de Chaumont who arranged his dinner parties, while one of the daughters did his household bookkeeping.

Word of his success among the ladies reached Philadelphia, where it aroused criticism in some circles. But, as he explained once to Jefferson, women felt free to pursue a man of his age—when you are safely past seventy, Franklin told Jefferson, you, too, will be pursued.

Temple was always good company, an amusing and animated young man, and beautifully dressed, for clothing was of great importance to him. He showed no interest in further education, and seemed to be fitting into his role as Franklin's personal secretary and aide. Benny went to a nearby boarding school, coming home once a week for Sunday dinner; in a brief letter to "My dear, dear Polly" soon after his arrival, Franklin said, "I have with me here my young grandson, Benjamin Franklin Bache, a special good boy. I shall give him a little French language . . . and then send him over to pay his respects to Miss Hewson. My love to all that love you." Despite his poor record as a matchmaker, Franklin could not resist pairing three-year-old Eliza Hewson with Benny, age seven.

After two years of boarding school near Passy, he decided the Kingbird ought to have a Protestant education, and sent him to a school in Geneva, Switzerland. The boy was still shy, and in Switzerland he became very quiet, a silent sufferer who longed for companionship.

In the neighborhood, and forming part of the circle that wel-

WORD OF HIS SUCCESS
AMONG THE LADIES
REACHED PHILADELPHIA,
WHERE IT AROUSED
CRITICISM IN SOME CIRCLES.

comed Franklin to Passy, were two women with whom he developed
close friendships that were half flirtation. Madame Brillon was a talented musician and composer in her early thirties, married to a
treasury official many years older; John Adams believed she was one
of the most beautiful women in Paris. She called Franklin "mon
cher Papa," my dear father, and consulted him about her personal
problems as she had once consulted her own father. But there was a
difference. As she told Franklin, "People have the audacity to criti-
cize my pleasant habit of sitting on your knee."

The other was Madame Helvétius, the widow of a distinguished philosopher; close to sixty, a great beauty in her youth,
she was now animated, impulsive, the vibrant center of a group
that brought together some of Europe's leading intellectuals. To
Franklin, she represented the finest sort of independent woman.

When John Adams brought his wife, Abigail, to Paris a few
years later, she saw Madame Helvétius in a different light, colored
by her own opinion of Franklin, whom she called "The Old De-
ceiver"—believing him to be jealous, greedy, and immoral.

When they went into the room to dine, Mrs. Adams began,
Madame Helvétius

was placed between [Doctor Franklin] and Mr. Adams. She carried on the chief of the conversation at dinner, frequently lock-
ing her hand into the Doctor's, and sometimes spreading her
arms upon the backs of both the gentlemen's chairs, then
throwing her arm carelessly upon the Doctor's neck . . . I was

highly disgusted, and never wish for an acquaintance with ladies of this cast. After dinner, she threw herself on a settee, where she showed more than her feet. She had a little lap-dog, who was, next to the Doctor, her favorite. This she kissed, and when he wet the floor she wiped it up with her chemise. This is one of the Doctor's most intimate friends, with whom he dines once every week, and she with him.

Franklin's friendship with Madame Helvétius began with their first meeting, and before long he was pressing her to marry him— perhaps seriously, always in an elegantly humorous vein that might have been his way of protecting himself against rejection.

Surely the most extraordinary aspect of Franklin's Paris years was the love he inspired in rich and poor alike, a love that began before he set foot on French soil. In America, his scientific work had been accepted without any great excitement, and in England he was valued mostly by the Royal Society and the universities. But in France Franklin was larger than life—a scientist, a thinker, a hero. Crowds lined the streets the day he arrived in Paris. Within weeks it seemed that every mantelpiece in the city displayed an engraving of his face, and after two years it was everywhere—on snuffboxes, bracelets, rings, watches, clocks, vases, dishes, handkerchiefs, pocketknives, even, somehow, on hats and coats.

Adams, who was no admirer of Franklin, found that Franklin's name was known "to government and people, to kings, courtiers, nobility, clergy and philosophers . . . to such a degree that there is scarcely a peasant or a citizen, a lady's chambermaid or a scullion in the kitchen who was not familiar with it and who did not consider him a friend to humankind. When they spoke of him, they seemed to think he was to restore the golden age."

Men carried canes because Franklin used a cane. In the town of Nantes women wore wigs that were shaped like his marten fur cap, calling it a coiffure "à la Franklin." The Countess Diane de Polignac spoke of him so often and so ardently that the young King, Louis XVI, had a chamber pot made for her of Sèvres porcelain with Franklin's portrait at the bottom. To Baron Turgot, a financier and statesman, Franklin was the hero who had "snatched the lightning from the heavens, the scepter from tyrants." A print by the artist Jean-Honoré Fragonard showed a turbulent scene in the heavens, with anguished gods swirling around Franklin, while flashes of lightning threaten a majestic figure, America, crowned with stars. But there is nothing to fear, for Franklin (seated on a cloud, and wearing a Roman toga) deflects the lightning by holding aloft the shield of Minerva, goddess of wisdom.

To the man in the street he was Poor Richard, whose tight-fisted wisdom had been translated into French and sold as *The Way to Wealth* (reprinted four times in the next two years). Paris and the court saw him as a philosopher-king, his gray hair straggling and scanty where it escaped from under the fur hat. Imagine, people said, that such a man, a thinker, an immortal, should appear in the dress of a simple Quaker, for by now he was fully aware of the propaganda value of the fur cap and the plain clothing, and took pleasure in wearing them as often as possible.

And all this time the partnership between France and the re-bellious colonies remained a secret. Louis XVI, who had come to the throne in 1774, was still reluctant; he promised a loan of two million livres, which sounded grand but would not go far—and there were financiers like Turgot advising him that one more war would bankrupt the nation. (Turgot was right; it did.)

In Paris cafés, young gentlemen criticized General Washing-ton—inexperienced in military tactics, they said; already driven out of Long Island, leaving New York in the hands of the British. Yet they longed to join him, for it was part of the glamour surrounding Dr. Franklin that he represented a people who challenged the estab-lishment. On Franklin's orders the constitution he had written for Pennsylvania was translated into French and published, and words like "liberty" and "freedom" proved to be intoxicating, even though it was not entirely clear what they meant. When the Marquis de Lafayette, age nineteen, bought a ship, complete with captain and crew, and sailed off to fight beside Washington—although the King expressly forbade it—there were many who envied him.

There was a shortage of money. The commissioners—Franklin, Deane, and Lee—were already in debt. As Silas Deane put it in the autumn of 1777, "Our expenditures and engagements . . . far ex-ceeded our funds; and [there were] no remittances from America . . . It was proposed, even by Dr. Franklin, that we should dispose of part of the clothing provided [by France, to be sent to America], and of the ships engaged." The debts would have mattered less if the news from America had not continued to be uniformly bleak, with Washington losing almost every action he undertook.

Now a British army in New York was poised to go north, while in Canada another British army started south. When the two forces met, they would cut New England off from Philadelphia, signaling the beginning of the end of the rebellion. The plan might well have worked, except that the army starting from Canada, under the command of General John Burgoyne, ran short of supplies and waited in vain for the army from New York—which was not traveling north at all, but west toward Philadelphia, the capital of the new republic. Why?

Because they had never received an order to go north. They captured and occupied Philadelphia, where a British officer was lodged in the music room in company with Franklin's glass armonica and Sally's harpsichord. The Continental Congress fled to Baltimore, Maryland.

In Paris the commissioners heard news from America six to eight weeks after it happened, and by early December they knew only that Philadelphia was in danger. Hearing hoofbeats in the driveway at Passy, Franklin ran to the front entrance and shouted to the rider, "Sir, is Philadelphia taken?"

"It is, sir," came the reply, and as Franklin turned to go, the rider called after him, "But, sir, I have greater news than that. General Burgoyne and his whole army are prisoners of war."

Burgoyne had surrendered to the American general Horatio Gates, after a long-drawn-out battle at Saratoga, New York—where American troops used French guns and French ammunition, eight shiploads' worth that French ships had smuggled past the British blockade. Washington had a ship fitted out to carry the news to Franklin with the greatest possible speed, and it crossed the Atlantic in an amazing four weeks, arriving on December 4, 1777.

Franklin found it hard to believe: an army of almost ten thousand reduced to six thousand; six generals and three hundred officers handed over; the world's greatest power humbled by a ragtag army consisting mostly of militia—volunteer farmers. How to spread this astonishing news? Waiting for the Paris newspapers would take too long; so would printing up the story and having it distributed on handbills. The three commissioners therefore wrote a brief announcement beginning: "Burgoyne compelled to put down his arms, 9200 men killed or taken prisoner." Everyone they could lay hands on, including the man who had brought the message, Jonathan Loring Austin, was set to work copying the news out by hand. The message went mostly to officials, but sometimes found its way to ordinary men and women. It seemed to Temple that the French rejoiced as if the victory had been their own.

Franklin wrote immediately to Vergennes. Two days later he received a note from Louis XVI saying the King would no longer decline to hear any proposals the commissioners cared to put forward. Then several weeks went by while France conferred with its allies, notably Spain.

Now Franklin was bombarded with letters from across the English Channel asking—sometimes imploring—for peace. Peace on English terms, meaning something just short of independence yet infinitely better than colonial status. Bribes were offered: suppose the British created up to two hundred American peers, surely that would tempt him? What if Franklin and Deane were provided with safe-conduct passes to England, would they come for direct discussions of peace terms? Franklin angrily rejected it all.

In several cases the messages were delivered in person, one of them by an old and dear friend of Franklin's, James Hutton, who declared that there was in England such a powerful desire for peace "that anything short of absolute Independency almost would be practicable, and could take place." Franklin sent him home empty-handed; "absolute Independency" was all he would settle for.

In a letter to another British friend, Franklin spoke candidly about the country he had loved for most of his life: "I was fond to a folly of our British connection and it was with infinite regret that I saw the necessity you would force us into of breaking it. But the extreme cruelty with which we have been treated has now extinguished every thought of returning to it, and separated us forever. You have thereby lost limbs that will never grow again."

Although he made it clear to the British that he would not enter into negotiations without independence, Franklin did not make it clear to the French. They knew something was afoot, and he wanted them to know it—to be troubled by the serious possibility that America might return to the embrace of Great Britain.

In December, while Franklin, Lee, and Deane were meeting with Vergennes, an Englishman by the name of Paul Wentworth arrived in Paris. He was the chief of England's secret service in France, and his opening gambit was a note to Silas Deane saying that someone who wanted to meet Deane could be found at the public baths, or else at the Luxembourg Gallery; failing that, in a coach at a named place on the road to Passy. Deane very sensibly replied that anyone who wanted to see him would find him in his office.

When they met, Wentworth laid out a plan for reconciliation between Britain and America—the colonies to have their own congress, Parliament to concern itself only with trade and foreign policy; there would be peerages, positions, money, for anyone who helped bring about such an agreement.

Deane passed the message on to Franklin, who had no interest in meeting Wentworth. But when the commissioners learned that Spain had declined to join with France and America against England, Franklin did an about-face.

He consented to a meeting with Wentworth. At the same time he let word leak out that there was a British emissary in Paris working to reach an agreement with the Americans—and that this agreement could well include American help with the British effort to take over French islands in the Indies. The British representative was pressing him, Franklin said, for an answer. This information was rapidly transmitted to London by the network of English spies, as Franklin knew it would be.

At his meeting with Wentworth, Franklin was offered an unsigned letter that opened up the possibility of unqualified independence. According to Wentworth, Franklin said it was "a very interesting, sensible letter, and [he] applauded the candor, good sense and benevolent spirit of it." This was a good deal like the language Franklin might have used to compliment Benny Bache on a well-written letter.

Two days later Vergennes's secretary requested Franklin and the other two commissioners to answer, in writing, the following question: What must be done to ensure that they would not listen "to any propositions from England for a new Connection with that Country"?

The French must sign a treaty, Franklin said in reply, the same treaty the commissioners had been proposing since they first arrived—two treaties, actually, one creating a military alliance, the other related to friendship and trade. This was acceptable to the French, but with one requirement: before the two nations were knitted together, America must vow she would never make peace with Britain except with French consent. To this Franklin and the other commissioners agreed.

On February 6, 1778, Franklin, Deane, and Lee met with Conrad-Alexander Gerard, the representative of Vergennes, who had two treaties awaiting their signatures, one commercial, the other an alliance. All major questions having been settled by then, there were only minor matters to quibble about, and they did quibble—until the moment when Gerard took up his pen and signed. Then one by one the Americans signed, first Franklin, then Deane, then Lee. According to a later account by Temple, Franklin wore the same suit of Manchester velvet he had worn during his humiliation before Britain's Privy Council; he said he wanted it to have its revenge.

The final step in the treaty-making process would take place at Versailles, the splendid palace where Louis XVI lived, surrounded by his royal court. At long last the three American commissioners would be presented to the King, the treaties would be signed, and the English compelled to swallow the mixture.

Franklin had ordered a wig made for the occasion, but when it came it didn't seem to fit, so he decided to go without it, and without the customary dress sword. He wore a dark velvet suit, very plain but with the usual flurry of white ruffles at wrist and neck. (The whiteness of Franklin's ruffles and personal linen was legendary.) He had on white stockings and carried a white hat under his arm. One of the court ladies, the painter Élisabeth Vigée-Lebrun, saw him at the signing ceremony and looked him over with her practiced eye: "But for his noble face I should have taken him for a big farmer, so great was his contrast with the other diplomats, who were all powdered, in full dress, and splashed all over with gold and ribbons."

Vergennes presented Franklin to Louis XVI, who said, "Assure Congress of my friendship. I hope this will be for the good of the two nations." Franklin thanked him in the name of America: "Your Majesty may count on the gratitude of Congress and its faithful observance of the pledges it now takes."

The treaties, a personal triumph for Franklin, marked the beginning of his career as a diplomat. Until now he had been learning, waiting on events, but with the formation of the French-American alliance it would be up to him to keep supplies flowing across the Atlantic—money, ships, and fighting men; Deane and

Lee were useful but not necessary. As America's representative in France, chief adviser to America's navy, and her overseas financial officer, Franklin would be dealing with the Continental Congress, with Vergennes, and indirectly with the young King, as well as anybody and everybody who wanted to go to America. In some ways Franklin was well suited to this line of work, in others less so.

A diplomat, like a spy, must be able to conceal his feelings, and that was how Franklin had lived his life—with his feelings under wraps. Although he flirted outrageously, he never fell in love. He disliked argument and would go to great lengths to avoid it; when the Abbé Jean-Antoine Nollet attacked his electrical theories, Franklin thought of sending "a long, courteous letter" that would set the matter right, but then gave it up and did nothing. When his fellow commissioners riled him, he transformed his face into an expressionless mask, as he had in 1774 at the Cockpit.

To the French, who adored him, he showed his best self: an idealist, a lover of mankind. And this persona was just as genuine as the secret operative behind the wooden mask. That spring he wrote to a Boston clergyman:

All Europe is on our side . . . Those who live under arbitrary power do nevertheless approve of liberty, and wish for it; they almost despair of recovering it in Europe; they read the translations of our separate colony constitutions with rapture; and there are such numbers everywhere, who talk of removing to America, with their families and fortunes, as soon as peace and

our independence shall be established, that it is generally believed we shall have a prodigious addition of strength, wealth,
and arts, from the emigrations of Europe . . . Hence it is a common observation here that our cause is *the cause of all mankind*
and that we are fighting for their liberty in defending our own.

He believed that the young King Louis XVI was virtuous, that
the French were eager to help an infant nation, and if these views
were unrealistic they were also generous and likely to inspire gen-
erosity.

Now that the treaties were signed, Franklin waited. Across the
ocean Washington waited, and so did Lafayette, along with many
whose names have not survived. They were waiting to see how the
King of France would save the revolution.

Chapter Fifteen

Rough Beginnings

French sails appeared off the coast of
Maryland in the *summer of 1778* —
twelve heavy warships, called *ships of the line,*

and four frigates, which were also warships, but lighter. They were towing, as prizes of war, seven British vessels they had captured on the way. The admiral of this handsome fleet was Jean-Baptiste-Charles-Henri-Hector, Count d'Estaing, a distant relation of Lafayette's.

This was what Washington had been hoping for, a naval force powerful enough to attack New York harbor and blast the British out of the city. But no, Estaing saw that the harbor was too shallow for his ships—or else he lost his nerve at the last moment. When Washington proposed instead an attack on the British garrison at Newport, Rhode Island, Estaing was delighted. It would be a joint effort, he said, a joint command, France and America fighting side by side.

But the French officers were openly scornful of the New England militia, comparing them to barbarian hordes, and an ongoing dispute about which side deserved the honor of attacking first both amazed and disheartened Lafayette. When the French got word of a British fleet approaching—thirty ships coming from New York to defend the Newport garrison—Estaing and his fleet responded by sailing forth to meet and engage the enemy.

Shots were exchanged, a few opening fusillades, but then the sky grew dark. A powerful gale broke over both fleets, scattering ships, beating the French back toward land. The admiral's flagship was badly injured; his captains insisted the fleet must withdraw to Boston for repairs. Abandon the Americans? Alas, there was no help for it. As Estaing explained to Washington, he had promised

Louis XVI that in case of damage to the ships they would be taken
to a major shipyard for repairs. Dismay and anger among the Americans when they heard of it; accusations of cowardice, desertion.
What did a brisk wind and a few raindrops mean to fighting men?

But the French ships did pull out, and Lafayette sulked in what
had been the French officers' quarters; he was thoroughly ashamed
of the Americans' behavior, their taunting of valorous Frenchmen
who had traveled all that great distance to help them. There was
worse to come: reports of French sailors and marines insulted on the
streets of Boston, followed by duels and bloody riots. When Estaing
threw up his hands and decided to retreat to the West Indies,
Lafayette was so miserable that Washington sent him home on
leave.

More than two thousand volunteers simply walked out of the
American army after Estaing's unfortunate visit. This was how the
French-American alliance began, with bitterness and disillusion on
both sides—while in Paris, on a very small scale, the three commissioners were having disputes of their own. Arthur Lee, for example,
was a thorn in Franklin's side. Intelligent and well educated, Lee belonged to a prominent Virginia family; one of his many brothers was
to earn the nickname "Lighthorse Harry" for the success of the irregular cavalry unit he commanded during the revolution.

But Arthur was quarrelsome and subject to horrific fits of jeal-
ousy. When he was not accusing Franklin of greed and dishonesty,
he accused Silas Deane, in the most venomous terms, of outright
corruption.

After a series of letters had gone unanswered, Franklin wrote
to Lee:

> If I have often received and borne your . . . rebukes without re-
> ply, ascribe it to the right causes, my concern for the honor &
> success of our mission, which would be hurt by our quarrelling,
> my love of peace, my respect for your good qualities, and my
> pity of your sick mind, which is forever tormenting itself, with
> its jealousies, suspicions & fancies that others mean you ill,
> wrong you, or fail in respect for you. If you do not cure your self
> of this temper it will end in insanity, of which it is the symp-
> tomatic forerunner . . . God preserve you from so terrible an
> evil: and for His sake pray suffer me to live in quiet.

Because he had powerful friends in Congress, Lee managed to
have Deane called back to America for investigation—an event of
special significance because Deane's replacement was John Adams.
Forty-three years old, newly retired from the Continental Congress,
where he had served on ninety committees and headed twenty-five,
Adams was high-minded and hardworking. Armed with great energy
and great intellectual attainments, he would furnish Franklin with a
sort of honorable opposition in Paris, for they were very different.

Adams joined the household at Passy and immediately set to
work inspecting the business of the commission. Reading papers
and letters, he could find no system to them, no records, no files, no
order anywhere. It seemed to him that Franklin avoided everything

except the social engagements that kept him busy from morning to night—crowds of visitors coming, Adams said, "to see the great Franklin, and to have the pleasure of telling Stories about his Simplicity, his bald head and scattering strait hairs among their Acquaintances."

The man was "indolent," Adams concluded, using a pleasanter word for "lazy." He said he realized "the Business of our Commission would never be done, unless I did it."

There must have been some truth to these observations, since Franklin made them himself. In an essay called "Dialogue Between the Gout and Mr. Franklin," he imagined a conversation with his longtime companion, the Gout, who spoke sternly to him:

> Mr. F. "It is not fair to say I take no exercise, when I do very often, going out to dine and returning in my carriage."
>
> The Gout: "That, of all imaginable exercises, is the most slight and insignificant. By observing the degree of heat obtained by different kinds of motion, we may form an estimate of the quantity of exercise given by each. Thus, for example, if you turn out to walk in winter with cold feet, in an hour's time you will be in a glow all over; ride on horseback, the same effect will scarcely be perceived by four hours' round trotting; but if you loll in a carriage . . . you may travel all day and gladly enter the last inn to warm your feet by a fire. Flatter yourself then no longer that half an hour's airing in your carriage deserves the name of exercise."

Mr. F. "What then would you have me do with my carriage?"

The Gout: "Burn it if you choose; you may at least get heat out of it once in this way; or if you dislike that proposal, here's another for you; observe the poor peasants who work in the vineyards and grounds . . . four or five old men and women, bent and perhaps crippled by the weight of years."

Advise your coachman, the Gout continues, to take them home in the carriage. To which Mr. F. responds, "Your reasonings grow very tiresome."

About the business of the commission, there was a good deal of it that Franklin would have liked to ignore; although he was responsible for naval affairs, for example, he knew nothing about ships and never claimed to. Commercial transactions he had left to Silas Deane, who was cheated and swindled by the merchants he dealt with; it's not likely that Franklin could have done any better, partly because he avoided confrontation and always had, and partly also because his health was poor. He was troubled not only by gout but by that itchy affliction of the skin he called scurf, by kidney stones, which could be unspeakably painful, and most of all by old age. He was saving his energy for what mattered: France and the alliance.

And Adams was compelled to admit that, in spite of his many faults, Franklin had the confidence of Vergennes and the French court. One reason among many was that "indolence" of his—the appearance of having all the time in the world, which was exactly the style of the French aristocracy, and the opposite, as they saw it, of busy-ness. Members of the middle class—the bourgeoisie—were busy. Adams was obviously very busy. Franklin was, or seemed to be, pleasantly at leisure, happy to spend an hour with anyone who applied.

When the Congress decided that one commissioner was enough, Franklin was appointed that one commissioner, an arrangement Adams himself had suggested. Adams went home, troubled about his future. Arthur Lee was sent to Madrid. Unable to prove his innocence of financial fraud, Silas Deane never rejoined the commission. When he died some ten years later, his last remaining friend was Dr. Bancroft, the spy.

And Franklin remained in place, having increased in importance and responsibility. He negotiated another loan, this time for three million livres. To an English friend he wrote, "I do not find that I grow any older. Being arrived at seventy, and considering that by traveling further in the same road I should probably be led to the grave, I stopped short, turned about, and walked back again; which having done these four years, you may now call me sixty-six."

On the other side of the ocean, meanwhile, the Continental Congress told John Adams they wanted him back in Paris, this time as sole commissioner authorized to negotiate for peace with Great Britain. He had never asked for the post and was amazed when told about it, but in February of 1780 he set out obediently for France some three months after reaching home.

Adams's second visit to Paris was destined to be brief. It was his belief that Franklin was overly grateful to France, that "a little apparent stoutness and greater air of independence and boldness" in the commissioner's behavior would have better results. It was also his belief that Franklin's opinion of him, Adams, was colored by "sordid envy."

Whereas Franklin kept his feelings bottled up inside, Adams was entirely the opposite—his feelings escaped through every pore of his body. So his suspicions about the Count de Vergennes and the foreign ministry—his belief that when the war was over, French policy would be to keep America weak, to "Make us feel our obligations"—were heard by Vergennes as surely as if they had been spoken out loud. He continued writing to Vergennes frankly and explicitly "upon everything that appears to me to be of importance to the common cause"—until July 29, when Vergennes sent a note to Adams bluntly informing him, "The King does not need your solicitations to direct his attention to the interests of the United States."

Vergennes then turned to Franklin and told him "he would enter into no further discussions with Mr. Adams, nor answer any more of his letters." Franklin packed up all the papers connected with Adams's second stay in Paris and sent the lot to the Continental Congress, along with the information that "Mr. Adams has given extreme offense to the court here," followed by an account of his tactlessness.

Adams left Paris again, this time for Holland, to see "whether something might be done to render us less dependent on France."

Chapter Sixteen

Wounding of a Proud Man

When his leave was over, the Marquis de Lafayette came back to America with breathtaking news for George Washington.

Although the Count d'Estaing and his ships had never returned from the Indies, Louis XVI had promised a greater, more powerful fleet along with a body of ten thousand fighting men, both fleet and men to be commanded by Jean-Baptiste-Donatien de Vimeur, Count de Rochambeau. He was an experienced soldier, the descendant of many generations of soldiers who had been serving their country since the Crusades.

When the two leaders met, Washington unfolded his cherished plan for an all-out assault on New York, one that would bring the war to a triumphant conclusion. Rochambeau agreed that capturing New York would put an end to the war—but alas, their combined forces were not sufficient for such an attack; they would need another, even larger fleet, he said, and many more troops—he had barely five thousand men. He would remain in Newport with his ships until reinforcements arrived from the Indies, as they most assuredly would.

Washington and Rochambeau shook hands cordially, drank a toast to future victories, and then parted, each thinking his private thoughts. Washington was highly skeptical of French promises; he would believe in this great French fleet when he saw it. And Rochambeau must have wondered if America's revolution had already played itself out, for Washington's army amounted at best to three thousand gaunt and weary men, most of them dressed in little more than trousers and a thin linen jacket; nobody seemed to own even a pair of stockings.

Letters from home begged the soldiers for money to feed the children, but there was no money—the men were paid in Continental dollars, which were almost worthless. Charleston had fallen; two southern states, South Carolina and Georgia, were under British control; and the southern army hardly existed now. Washington's men felt neglected, cheated, and abused; many would rebel.

In Paris, with Adams gone, the life of the sole commissioner was considerably more peaceful, but with heavier demands on his time. Franklin had to be "ambassador, secretary, admiral, consular agent . . . besides an immense correspondence and acquaintance, each of which would be enough for the whole time of the most active men in the vigor of youth"—so Adams described Franklin's position to the Continental Congress. His tone was sympathetic, respectful; he was aware that Franklin felt overwhelmed.

There was no one to help him except for Temple, now about twenty years old. The flow across the Atlantic of arms, ammunition, and supplies continued, and bills that came from different ports and nations often required immediate payment. This meant being always at home, so Franklin was never free for a day's excursion into the country, "and the want of exercise has hurt our healths in several instances." Franklin always spoke of "us" now, meaning himself and Temple. "Temple is my right hand," he said. "Temple and I are perfect drudges."

He used a similar phrase in a letter to Sally about Benny, her son:

Ben writes to me often. He is very glorious at present, having obtained the Prize of his School for best Translation from the Latin into French; which was presented to him in the Cathe-

dral Church by the first Magistrate of the City. I send you his
Letter and his Master's containing the News of this Important
Event. He gives a Treat on the Occasion to the rest of the
Scholars for which I shall pay with much Pleasure . . . I continue
in health, but have too much to do.—The Congress have kept
me in constant Expectation of being assisted by a Secretary; but
he has not yet appeared, and Temple and I are absolute Drudges.

Although his grandson Benny wrote to him often, Franklin
rarely replied, and he never went to visit, never had the boy
brought to Passy for vacation. Richard Bache, Benny's father, said:
"It would give us pleasure to hear, that you had found leisure
enough to visit him at Geneva, but I suspect your time has been
more importantly employed."

Franklin wasn't writing to the Continental Congress either. He
didn't know why, only that he had developed an "aversion to writing" that was almost insurmountable. Even Vergennes, who liked
and respected Franklin, confessed to the French ambassador in
America that there were "important matters on which I see this
minister maintain silence whereas the good of the service requires
he transmit his opinion to Congress."

According to the French ambassador, the Congress believed
this failure to write showed that Franklin was devoting precious little time to public affairs. Furthermore, the ambassador said, only the
difficulty of finding a suitable successor had kept the Congress from
dismissing Franklin. Getting rid of him. Sending him packing.

He had been away from home now for twenty years—sixteen

on his two missions to England, four in France—so that people in the Congress, their views and needs and personal quirks, would have seemed distant to him, their faces hard to remember. To them, he must have seemed equally distant, more an idea than a person, with the added demerit of living on their money. Living very comfortably, some people said. In luxury, sin, and corruption, according to others.

Early in 1781 an earthquake erupted under Franklin's feet. It took the form of a letter from the Congress: Colonel John Laurens was on his way to Versailles as a special envoy, they said, bringing an urgent plea for a loan of twenty-five million livres—over and above the twenty-five million Franklin had won the year before. What was behind this? Franklin asked himself. How come Laurens, in his midtwenties, was given full ministerial powers to negotiate for a loan, when he should have come as an aide, as the secretary the Congress kept promising, or as a military adviser? And why was he, Franklin, being pushed aside? Because that's what it amounted to, pushing him aside, as if his own efforts were not enough.

But he already knew the answer, because his sister Jane and Sally's husband, Richard Bache, kept him abreast of Philadelphia politics. From them he learned that Arthur Lee and Lee's brother Henry, a congressman, had been carrying on a congressional campaign against Franklin. They were "very laborious," Jane said, "to make people believe you have done something criminal in money matters." A motion to recall him had been placed before the Congress, she went on. Although it failed this time, another time it might not fail—some of the "dirt will stick," she said.

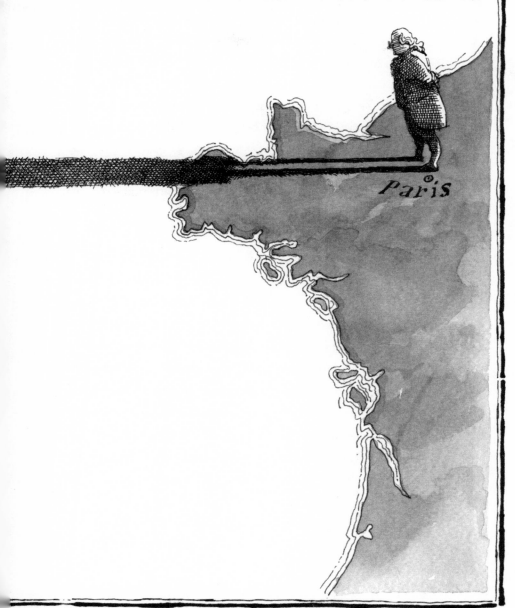

There were people who claimed that Franklin was so smitten with the charms of Paris and its women that he neglected his duties; others pointed to Temple, the son of a loyalist, now acting as Franklin's confidential secretary, who could very well be spying for the British.

"Methinks it is rather some merit that I have rescued a valuable young man from the danger of being a tory," Franklin wrote to Bache. "It is enough that I have lost my son, would they add my grandson? An old man of seventy, I undertook a winter voyage at the command of the Congress . . . with no other attendant to take care of me. I am continued here in a foreign country, where, if I am sick, his filial attention comforts me."

If the Congress told him to send Temple away, he wouldn't do it. He explained to Sally that he would rather resign than be separated from Temple. Perhaps it would be wise to resign in any case, before he was thrown overboard. Because he was old and sick and deeply wounded, needing a way out that saved what remained of his dignity, he composed a letter of resignation without the faintest hint of bitterness: "I have been engaged in public affairs . . . during the long term of fifty years, an honour sufficient to satisfy any reasonable ambition, and I have no other [ambition] left but that of repose."

His one request, the single favor he asked of the Congress, was that they take Temple under their protection:

I have educated him from his Infancy, and I brought him over with an Intention of placing him where he might be qualified for the Profession of the Law; but the constant Occasion I had for his Service as a private Secretary during the time of the Commissioners, and more extensively since their Departure, has induced me to keep him always with me; and indeed being continually disappointed of the Secretary Congress had at different Times intended me it would have been impossible for me without this young Gentleman's Assistance, to have gone through the Business incumbent on me! He has . . . lost so much of the time necessary for Law Studies, that I think it rather advisable for him to continue . . . in the line of public foreign Affairs, for which he seems qualified by a Sagacity, & Judgment above his Years, great Diligence and Activity, exact Probity, a genteel Address, a Facility in Speaking well the French Tongue . . . After all the Allowance I am capable of making for the Partiality of a Parent to his Offspring, I cannot but think he may in time make a very able foreign Minister for the Congress.

So Franklin said, and sincerely believed.

He had been instructed by the Congress not to wait for the special envoy, Colonel Laurens, but to proceed with earnest requests to Vergennes for money, and Franklin wrote to the foreign minister as he had so many times before:

I am grown old . . . and it is probable I shall not long have any more concern in these affairs. I therefore take this occasion to express my opinion to your Excellency, that the present conjuncture is critical; that there is some danger lest the Congress should lose its influence over the people, if it is found unable to procure the [funds] that are wanted. And that the whole system of the new government in America may thereby be shaken.

If England recovers her American colonies, those fertile and extensive regions and vast seacoast, he went on, she will become the "*terror of Europe*," able to "exercise with impunity that insolence, which is so natural to their nation, and which will increase enormously with the increase of their power."

Because France was close to bankruptcy, this request for money, coming so soon after the earlier gift, was shocking to Vergennes. But he transmitted the message to Louis XVI, using several of Franklin's arguments, and the King agreed—Franklin was to have six million livres, not as a loan but as a gift. A gift to General Washington, that was how the King put it, the money to be kept in a special account in Washington's name so that he alone could draw on it.

Franklin wrote to the President of the Congress to tell him about the gift, and in the same post sent his letter of resignation, with his assurances that he had never for one moment lost faith in America's "glorious cause." He would have to wait two to four months for a reply.

While he waited, life in America's army grew increasingly desperate. Pennsylvania and New Jersey regiments rebelled, killing two officers; Washington ordered their commanders to force an unconditional surrender and execute some of the leaders. Accordingly, the two ringleaders were tied to a fence and shot at close range by a firing squad, their heads shattered to bits. This was done to compel loyalty, but only a few weeks later there was another mutiny, and then another in May. Lafayette wrote to Franklin, "We are naked, shockingly naked. No cloth to be got. No money . . . You have no idea of the shocking situation the Army is in." Washington wrote to Franklin to tell him America must have peace—or money.

Four days after Louis XVI agreed to the gift for Washington, John Laurens arrived at Versailles. He proved to be a fine-looking young man whose movements were brisk and quick, better suited to an army encampment than the elaborate politeness of Europe's most elegant court. He spoke fluent French. His father, Henry, had served for a year as President of the Continental Congress but was now under lock and key in the Tower of London, having been captured by British forces at sea.

Laurens brought with him an official letter from the Congress to the King, and another from Washington to Franklin—who saw, at a glance, that it was an attempt to console him. Just as he had suspected, in sending young Laurens, Congress was pushing aside old Franklin. "I can with pleasure add assurances of his attachment to you personally," Washington said, "and of his perfect disposition to conform to his instructions by availing himself of your advice & assistance upon all occasions."

A letter from Lafayette, a few weeks later, had the same intention of soothing Franklin's wounds: "That You Have Ennemies at

Philadelphia Both Within and Without doors is a thing to be Expected . . . I hope I need not Mentioninning to you that You Have in Congress as Well as Every Where Many faithfull friends, and thus the People at large Have a due Sence of theyr obligations to, and A proper Affectionate Respect for the Name of doctor franklin."

Laurens's petition to the King called for immediate aid in money—a loan of twenty-five million livres—as well as ammunition, military supplies, clothing, tents, and especially ships, enough ships to ensure naval supremacy in American waters. It was the task of young Laurens to place before the court his own authentic, first-hand account of American army life as it was being lived so that the French would see and hear the urgency of his mission.

During the next six weeks he went from Vergennes at Versailles to Franklin at Passy, then again to Vergennes—back and forth, back and forth without result, until, on impulse, he appealed directly to the King. This was a profound breach of etiquette, mortifying to Franklin, and Laurens apologized profoundly. But when he sailed for Boston, Laurens was able to take with him—in cash, and thanks to the King—part of the six million livres promised to Franklin for Washington. Another part went to Holland to be shipped from there, and military supplies were on order in France. Moreover, a loan of ten million livres from Holland, if it could be borrowed on French security, would also follow. And the fleet that would guarantee naval supremacy along America's coast? That, too, was on its way, commanded by a very tall man, Admiral François-Joseph-Paul, Count de Grasse.

Franklin survived the success of young Laurens with grace;

writing to Lafayette in mid-May, he said, "I think it was a wise measure to send Colonel Laurens here, who could speak knowingly of the state of the army . . . He has fully justified your character of him, & returns thoroly possessed of my esteem . . . This court continues firm in its friendship & does everything it can for us. Can we not do a little more for ourselves?"

His own fate was less bleak now, for the Congress had refused to accept his resignation. Furthermore, they told him he was appointed to be one of five commissioners who would negotiate a peace treaty. Franklin had no way of knowing there had been furious contention about his place on the peace commission. Only four states voted to include him with John Adams and the lawyer John Jay on a three-member board, but a compromise was suggested: expanding the number to five so that they could add Thomas Jefferson and Henry Laurens (in the hope that the latter would soon be released through a prisoner exchange), as well as Franklin. It was said he would have missed even being on the expanded list but for pressure applied by representatives of Vergennes.

He had survived, if only by a hair's breadth, but he had been gravely injured. Hearing that Robert Morris was named superintendent of finance, Franklin wrote to congratulate him—a prosperous Philadelphia merchant, Morris had served with Franklin on several congressional committees—and added a warning that should have scorched the page:

> You are wise in estimating beforehand, as the principal Advantage you can expect, the Consciousness of having done Service

to your Country. For the Business you have undertaken is of so complex a Nature, and must engross so much of your Time & Attention, as necessarily to hurt your private Interests; and the Publick is often niggardly even of its Thanks, while you are sure of being censured by malevolent Cricks and Bug Writers, who will abuse you while you are serving them, and wound your Character in nameless Pamphlets, thereby resembling those little, dirty, stinking Insects that attack us only in the dark, disturb our Repose, molesting & wounding us while our Sweat and Blood are contributing to their Subsistence.

Less than a year and a half after sailing home from France, Colonel John Laurens was killed in a skirmish in the low country of South Carolina; he was twenty-eight years old.

Chapter Seventeen

"Oh, God! It's all over!"

Yorktown, Virginia, October 16, 1781: After seven days and nights under fire, the British General Lord Cornwallis made a risky decision.

Rather than wait to be rescued, he would do the rescuing himself—bring out his men and lead them by forced march toward British headquarters in New York.

He knew the odds were against him, but he also knew he was trapped, the enemy having pinned him in place between land forces and sea forces. This French-American enemy had more than a hundred heavy guns firing at point-blank range. "The whole peninsula trembles under the incessant thunderings of our infernal machines," an American doctor wrote. Bodies and parts of bodies lay on the ground. In what passed for a sick bay, British soldiers were dying of smallpox.

Cornwallis had sent a message the day before to his commander, Sir Henry Clinton, in New York: "My situation now becomes very critical . . . The safety of the place is . . . so precarious that I cannot recommend that the fleet and army should run great risk in endeavoring to save us." There was no need for this warning. Cornwallis had believed he could always leave Yorktown under the protection of a British fleet, but Clinton was hesitant, overly concerned with safety, and he found serial excuses for not sending a fleet and army to Virginia.

The following were the land forces arrayed against Cornwallis: Rochambeau's French troops; America's Virginian troops under Lafayette and Anthony Wayne; and George Washington's New York contingent, altogether twenty-one thousand allied soldiers. Cornwallis had eight thousand.

The forces at sea consisted of a powerful fleet, the one

Rochambeau had told Washington to expect: twenty-eight warships, led by the giant *City of Paris*, with 110 guns; also a number of frigates, and some armed merchantmen, the whole under the command of the Count de Grasse. De Grasse was well over six feet tall, and on his first meeting with Washington had embraced him heartily in the French style, calling him "my dear little general."

De Grasse had sailed up from the Indies to position his ships at the entrance to Chesapeake Bay, a narrow waterway that formed the coastline of Virginia. When a British fleet appeared on the horizon, de Grasse sailed forth to meet them, attacking and mauling several of their ships until they limped away. Now the French were in command of the Chesapeake. Their presence prevented any attempt to resupply or rescue Cornwallis as surely as it prevented Cornwallis from leaving.

What he planned instead was a nighttime escape by water, on a route that avoided de Grasse and the Chesapeake. His headquarters in the little village of Yorktown faced French and American batteries on the landward side, while on the other side, east of the town, was the York River. Across the river, in an area called Gloucester Point, lay a British outpost guarded by some Virginia militia and about seven hundred French troops.

He would ferry his men over the river to Gloucester, using sixteen sturdy, oversize rafts; some of them were now bobbing at the river's edge, in the care of Royal Navy sailors. Once across, they would either meet Clinton's rescue ships—or else brush aside the small enemy force, and at first light next morning break out of the

Gloucester lines to head north. Living off the country, making for the mouth of the Delaware River, they could easily contact British forces in New York.

In theory this could work. By making three trips, the sixteen rafts could transport all British forces across the river well before morning. A number of rafts had already taken off and would return for a second load about two hours later. Now the Royal Welsh Fusiliers were boarding, and the Foot Guard, an elite unit. Cornwallis had trouble seeing their faces in the dark, but their voices seemed cheerful enough. He heard them jostling to arrange themselves so that each man took up the least possible share of space—arms folded across chests, elbows hugged tight to the body. He hoped he could bring them back safely to their parents and wives. He hoped they would live to fight other wars. Or not fight, just march handsomely in parades.

If it had been possible to look into his heart of hearts, it might have been seen that General Lord Cornwallis was not single-mindedly in support of this war. Fifteen years earlier, in the House of Lords, he was one of four peers who voted against Parliament's right to tax the American colonies—because "taxation and representation are inseparably united," a position founded "on the laws of nature for whatever is a man's own is absolutely his own." The words were not Cornwallis's, but he had voted for them. Why was he fighting in this war? Perhaps out of a sense of duty to his ancestors, who had fought for centuries in England's wars. Partway through the revolution, he had tried to resign but was not allowed to.

He judged it must be close to midnight, although the skies were so clouded over it was hard to tell. Still facing the river, he felt a raindrop on the side of his face, and a little stirring of breeze. Moments later there was a wrenching sound, like a convulsion of the heavens. Winds came from nowhere to whip the trees, bending them in half, and it seemed to happen within minutes, the rafts crashing against the shore, the men who had been waiting to board them shivering uncontrollably. How long would it last?

It lasted less than three hours, but by then it was too late to get the rest of the army across before daylight—the allies, in fact, were already alerted. The rafts that had left for Gloucester were coming soggily back now, under rifle fire.

Early next morning Cornwallis summoned his senior officers to discuss the fate of the British army. They had about a hundred mortar shells left; after that, they would be defenseless. What should I do? Cornwallis asked his officers. Fight to the last man? The officers said no. All of them said it. But even if they hadn't, Cornwallis would have said it for them.

About an hour later, a small, redcoated figure appeared on top of a low wall at the center of the British lines—a drummer boy, beating his drum. But with the constant firing, no one heard the drumbeat. Then a redcoated officer appeared beside the wall, carrying a white handkerchief and walking toward the American lines. One by one the guns fell silent; the drummer boy climbed down to walk next to the officer and continued to beat out his message. It was an invitation for the two parties to parley—to talk to each other.

On October 19, 1781, Cornwallis, Washington, and Rochambeau signed the draft of a surrender document. At about the same
time, Sir Henry Clinton and six thousand soldiers sailed from New
York harbor to rescue Cornwallis. Later that day, in a nearby
meadow, British troops marched out to give up their weapons. At
their head rode Brigadier General Charles O'Hara, Cornwallis's second in command, for Cornwallis could not bring himself to take
part in this ceremony of surrender.

Allied soldiers stood at attention on either side of the road
that led from Yorktown to Williamsburg. Marching between them,
the British soldiers kept their eyes fixed on the French, doing their
best not to see the Americans—as if they were surrendering only
to the French. And when O'Hara, leading the British line, finally reached the allied generals, he offered Cornwallis's sword to
Rochambeau as representing the surrender of the entire army; at the
same time he conveyed Cornwallis's regret that he was too sick to
attend the ceremonies himself. Rochambeau, smiling slightly and
shaking his head, motioned across the road to Washington. O'Hara
turned to offer excuses and the sword to Washington, who instructed him to give the weapon to General Benjamin Lincoln, the
American second in command.

Four weeks later all of Europe knew. "Oh, God! It's all over!"
cried the British Prime Minister. There was a widespread perception
that it truly was all over, that the British were increasingly unwill-
ing to hurl troops, weapons, and money down a bottomless pit on
the far side of a great ocean. Nevertheless, the American revolution
would limp along for two more years.

ROCHAMBEAU, SMILING SLIGHTLY
AND SHAKING HIS HEAD, MOTIONED ACROSS
THE ROAD TO WASHINGTON.
O'HARA TURNED TO OFFER EXCUSES AND
THE SWORD TO WASHINGTON, WHO
INSTRUCTED HIM TO GIVE THE WEAPON
TO GENERAL BENJAMIN LINCOLN,
THE AMERICAN SECOND IN COMMAND.

France paid for the victory at Yorktown. American losses were 22 killed, 56 wounded, but French losses were 52 killed, 134 wounded. And while it was done for their own reasons, reasons that had nothing to do with freedom or self-government, it was the French who paid for the revolution. During the years from 1779 to 1783, France lent twenty-one million livres, gave six million, and guaranteed another ten million. Apart from the loan guarantee obtained by John Laurens, the financial backing was entirely Franklin's work.

Chapter Eighteen

Making Peace

News of the victory at Yorktown reached
Versailles in mid-November, and all
of France burst into fireworks. Paris enjoyed

fireworks displays three nights in a row. A master pastry maker created "anti-English" bonbons and used confectioner's sugar to sculpt scenes of the British surrender. Fireworks in Bordeaux, it was said, brought on a kind of "delerium" that continued for weeks.

Benjamin Franklin's reaction was cautious; on the evening the news came, a visiting American found him "in an ecstacy of Joy." But when writing to Madame Brillon, who was spending the winter in Nice, he said nothing about Yorktown. She reproached him for it, and he reminded her that war, like chess, was full of uncertainty—when his luck was bad, he hoped for better luck; when it was good, he feared a change. To an English friend who sympathized with the American cause, he said, "I wish most heartily with you that this cursed War was at an End: But I despair of seeing it finished in my Time. Your thirsty Nation has not drank enough of our Blood."

In Parliament it would take at least two months for the party in power to be voted out and replaced by the opposition—only then could there be serious talk about peace. Franklin was enjoying a period of comparative calm. When English and French acquaintances asked for books about the New World, he sought them out and forwarded them. With a Scottish surgeon, Alexander Small, he discussed the ventilation of buildings, especially hospitals, and Small wrote several papers based in part on Franklin's ideas. With Marie-Antoinette's physician he discussed "the length of time during which the Power of Infection may be continued in dead Bodies," and sent on to him a paper of Dr. Small's. With another Frenchman, Franklin discussed linguistics by way of the language of the Delaware Indians. He exchanged letters with Jan Ingenhousz in Vienna on conduction in metals. Writing to Baron Turgot, he began, "I did intend when in London to have published a Pamphlet describing the new Stove you mention, and for that purpose had a Plate engraved of which I send you an Impression . . . I think with you that it is capable of being used to Advantage in our Kitchens, if one could overcome the Repugnance of Cooks to the using of new Instruments & new Methods." There was much more. He had become a one-man clearinghouse for books and ideas, a central reference point.

Of the five peace commissioners selected by the Continental Congress, two were unable to serve at all, Jefferson because his wife was dying, and Henry Laurens, the father of John, because he was still imprisoned in the Tower of London. Of the remaining three, John Adams was in The Hague, negotiating a commercial treaty with Holland, and John Jay remained in Madrid, where he had spent two years trying in vain for a Spanish alliance.

Franklin wrote back and forth to Adams, who warned that the French could not be trusted and said the same repeatedly in letters to Jay. Franklin saw matters differently: "This is really a generous Nation," he said, "fond of Glory and particularly that of protecting the Oppressed . . . Telling them their *Commerce* will be advantaged by our Success, and that it is their *Interest* to help us, seems as much as to say, Help us and we shall not be Obliged to you." He noted that General Cornwallis had arrived in England: "He seems to mix as naturally with that polluted Court as Pitch with Tar. There is no being in Nature too base for them to associate with, provided it may be thought capable of serving their Purposes."

In March 1782 Franklin learned that the British cabinet—the new, Whig cabinet—was sending an envoy to sound him out. His name was Richard Oswald; he was a retired Scots businessman who had dealt in army supplies and slaves and had lived for a time in America. When Oswald reached Paris, he proved to be older than Franklin by a year; relaxed and easygoing, with one good eye, he had an air of "great simplicity and honesty," Franklin said, sending him back to England with an official letter: the commission was ready to talk about peace, but only a peace based on independence.

Oswald returned to Paris in April, and this time brought official instructions to conclude a peace based on independence. It was also in April that Temple Franklin was appointed secretary to the peace commission. People said he was a dandy and a fop, a man-about-town and nothing more, but Franklin had pressed for Temple's appointment, and eventually the Congress agreed.

John Jay arrived in June, a tall, slender man with a patrician manner. His two fruitless years in Spain had left him nervous, at times extremely suspicious not only of Spain but also of France. Franklin told him they were under strict orders from the Congress "to make the most candid . . . communications upon all subjects to the ministers of our generous ally, the King of France," and to do nothing without their knowledge. America, in other words, was to move toward peace only in lockstep with France. Jay objected bit-

AMERICA, IN OTHER WORDS,
WAS TO MOVE TOWARD PEACE ONLY IN
LOCKSTEP WITH FRANCE.

terly to these orders, and Adams was outraged when he heard by letter—had they fought a war for independence, only to be ordered about by others? Adams said he would rather resign from the commission. Franklin countered: "It is our firm connection with France that gives us weight with England, and respect throughout Europe."

When the British envoy Oswald came again, he brought a second envoy, a much younger man probably chosen for his no-nonsense approach; he would keep Oswald reined in. But then Franklin's health broke down; he was suffering from kidney stones, an affliction that accompanied him to his deathbed. Adams was still in Holland, and Jay had to carry on alone—nervous, at times frightened, occasionally near panic. Little was accomplished.

By October, Franklin had essentially recovered. Adams arrived, reluctant to be there because Paris meant Franklin. It was Adams's belief that Franklin had blackened his reputation—when sending his papers to the Continental Congress (as it was his duty to do), Franklin chose to include with them an account of how Adams had offended Vergennes. This was not required; he did it out of irritation or impatience, or both. What was his opinion of Adams? "I am persuaded," he said once, "that he means well for his country, is always an honest man, often a wise one, but sometimes, and in some things, absolutely out of his senses."

Adams found lodgings in Paris on the Right Bank, near the Louvre, and put off calling on Franklin as long as he decently could, perhaps longer. At last it could be postponed no more: "That I have no friendship for Franklin I avow. That I am incapable of having any with a man of his moral sentiments I avow. As far as fate shall compel me to sit with him in public affairs, I shall treat him with decency and perfect impartiality."

He called on Franklin at Passy and spent several hours with him, praising Jay for his "firmness" and repeating his own accusations against the French. He said later that Franklin "heard me patiently but said nothing."

There they were, the three of them—Franklin, Adams, and Jay—expected to work productively together even though two of them were suspicious and resentful. For the most part they succeeded—not because they learned to love or even like one another, but because it was their duty. For both Franklin and Adams, public duty was one of life's compelling forces. But it was also true that under the surface of "decency and perfect impartiality" suspicion continued to smolder.

A prime source of discord was Franklin's desire to keep Vergennes, the French foreign minister, informed every step of the way. It was what the Congress wanted, what the French expected, and what Franklin believed they deserved. But he also knew his first duty lay with America. One day he faced up to that realization, and when the three of them were alone he said, "I am of your opinion and will go on with these gentlemen in the business without consulting this [the French] Court." Perhaps Vergennes learned about the agreement—Adams believed he did—but the work of the commission proceeded from then on with no major stumbling blocks.

Franklin had put together a memorandum he hoped would be

the basis for their talks, consisting of necessary points and advisable ones. Necessary points began with full and complete independence, went on to the settlement of all boundaries, and concluded with freedom of fishing on the Grand Banks off Newfoundland. Advisable points: American ships and trade to be put on an equal footing with British ships and trade, Britain to give up to America every part of Canada, voluntary reparations to be paid to those ruined by the war, and a public statement to be made by Parliament acknowledging the injuries done by Britain—"A few kind words would go far." No one but Franklin could have written that last sentence, with its commonplace directness and good sense.

With independence already agreed upon, the next matter of importance was drawing the boundaries of the new nation. The Americans wanted everything between the Appalachian Mountains and the Mississippi River, and the British agreed—which astounded the Americans. With a single stroke the commissioners had pretty much doubled the territory of the new nation. Would everything else be so easy?

Canada was not, the British flatly refusing to give it up. A fiery speech by Adams persuaded the others that Americans had the right to continue fishing off the Grand Banks. But the status of loyalists was more complex. Some eighty thousand had been driven out of their homes and compelled to flee to England. They were penniless, their farms and plantations having been confiscated, and now the British were saying in effect, Who's going to take care of them? Not us, we never wanted a revolution.

Jay and Adams had little sympathy for loyalists but might have been persuaded to soften their position rather than endanger the treaty. It was Franklin who cried out against them, Franklin who saw the loyalists as stained with the blood of innocents: Suppose we list the lootings, burnings, and scalpings carried out during the last years of the war by British troops and their Indian allies, he said, and compare them item by item with the sufferings of the loyalists. We'll see which side deserves compensation. Adams was amazed at the tenacity of the old man. He was implacable; he could not be moved.

While these discussions were taking place, William Franklin was on his way to England on a British warship. As president of the Board of Associated Loyalists, he was going to argue this same case for compensation in a British court. Imprisoned early in the war, he had been given a good deal of freedom, lodged in private homes in Connecticut, for example, and allowed to ride through the country-side in his own carriage. But he made contact with high-level British officers, and when Washington heard of it, he had William marched to the town of Litchfield while sick with fever and thrown into a dark, filthy cell. Totally isolated from the world, William was unable even to write a letter. He heard that his wife, Elizabeth, was seriously ill, perhaps dying, and begged for permission to see her; while the Congress thought it over at great length, Elizabeth died alone, among strangers, in a country that was foreign to her. William believed the cause was a broken heart.

Congress eventually arranged for an exchange of prisoners that set William free. On fire with stored-up anger, he made for British-held New York, threw himself into the loyalist struggle, and led innumerable guerrilla-style operations along the rebel coasts. The British were annoyed by these tactics, which they saw as mismanaged. Franklin was horrified by the bloodshed and violence William unleashed against his own countrymen.

After much debate, the question of compensation for loyalists was finally answered by leaving it up to the individual states. They did what was expected of them, essentially nothing.

Now a provisional treaty brought from London was signed in Oswald's hotel room; it would take effect only after France and Great Britain agreed on peace terms. Franklin sent a copy to Vergennes, thereby revealing to him that a good deal had been going on without the knowledge and cooperation of the French. But Vergennes said nothing to Franklin, at this point; he was aware of the pressure exerted by Adams and Jay.

There was more to come. For some time now Franklin had been waiting for a French loan, the amount not yet fixed. He had reminded the Congress that there were bounds to everything, that the resources of the French nation were not without limits. Americans ought to do more for themselves, he said; it was absurd that they pretended to be lovers of liberty while they grudged paying for the defense of it. Now he sent a note to Vergennes, informing him that an American ship, provided with a British safe-conduct pass and carrying dispatches for the Congress, was ready to sail: "I hoped I might have been able to send part of the [funds] we have asked, by this safe vessel . . . I fear the Congress will be reduced to despair when they find that nothing is yet obtained."

Vergennes did not erupt in anger. But his reply might have been spoken from behind clenched teeth:

> You have concluded your preliminary articles without any communications between us, although the instructions from Congress prescribe that nothing shall be done without the participation of the King . . . You are wise and discreet, sir; you perfectly understand what is due to propriety; you have all your life performed your duties. I pray you to consider how you fulfill those which are due to the King . . . When you shall be pleased to relieve my uncertainty I will entreat the King to enable me to answer your demands.

Translated into ordinary language, Vergennes was saying, Explain yourself or there will be no money.

Franklin gave it a good deal of thought. When he had composed a reply, he showed it to his fellow commissioners before sending it to Vergennes. You are quite right that in not consulting you we have been guilty of a breach of manners, he said, and for this he apologized. Then: "The English, I just now learn, flatter themselves they have already divided us. I hope this little misunderstanding will therefore be kept a secret, and that they will find themselves totally mistaken."

By bringing up the English desire to divide the French-

American allies, Franklin was reminding Vergennes that it could be done—that England wanted it done. England and America had much in common, starting with a language and customs, and it was in England's interest to push the French away (once the war was over) and to do business with its former colony, growing richer and more powerful in the process. For the same reason it was against the best interests of France to drive the other two closer together.

To Vergennes, this letter of Franklin's was so astonishing that he sent a copy to the French ambassador in Philadelphia, adding, "I think it proper that the most influential members of Congress should be informed of the very irregular conduct of their commissioners in regard to us." But then he changed course, told the ambassador not to pursue the matter, and even provided Franklin with a first installment of the badly needed funds—six hundred thousand livres, with more to follow, to a total of six million. Vergennes must have decided the matter was not worth wrangling over at that point.

And all along, Adams continued to resent the French. It was this total lack of gratitude Franklin found hard to accept. In connection with the treaty, he said that Adams

> thinks the French Minister one of the greatest Enemies of our Country, that he would have [narrowed] our Boundaries, to prevent the Growth of our People; contracted our Fishery, to obstruct the Increase of our Seamen . . . that to think of Gratitude to France is the greatest of Follies, and that to be influenced by

it would ruin us . . . the Instances he supposes of their ill will to us, which I take to be as imaginary as I know his Fancies to be, that Count de V. and myself are continually plotting against him, and employing the News-Writers of Europe to depreciate his Character, &c.

When the peace treaty was finally, formally signed in Paris, on September 3, 1783, it was the opinion of Vergennes that the three commissioners had obtained far more from the British than he had ever thought possible. In Franklin's words, "The great and hazardous enterprise we have been engaged in, is, God be praised, happily completed; an event I hardly expected I should live to see."

The news was heard in Haiti, where France ruled over an island population of black slaves who were worked in the sugar cane fields until they fell to the ground and died there. It was heard in Ireland, Russia, Poland, and Hungary, as well as in France itself. Wherever people longed to breathe free, the story of America's revolution brought a new and unsettling sense of possibility.

Chapter Nineteen

Coming Home

In June of 1783, when the brothers Joseph and Jacques Montgolfier sent up the world's first hot-air balloon in the south of France, Franklin could only read about it. But in August the world's second balloon made an ascent over Paris, and he joined the thousands who came to watch and marvel.

The first balloon had been made of linen, the hot air that filled it produced by burning straw. This time the balloon was varnished silk, with an extra shine to it because of a light rain; instead of hot air, it was filled with hydrogen gas made by pouring oil of vitriol on iron filings. "At 5 o Clock Notice was given to the Spectators by the Firing of two Cannon, that the Cord was about to be cut"—so Franklin described the spectacle to Sir Joseph Banks of the Royal Society. "And presently the Globe was seen to rise, and that as fast as a Body of 12 feet diameter with a force only of 39 pounds, could be supposed to move the resisting Air out of its way. There was some Wind, but not very strong. A little Rain had wet it, so that it shone, and made an agreeable Appearance. It diminished in Apparent Magnitude as it rose, till it entered the Clouds, when it seemed to me scarce bigger than an Orange."

Forty-five minutes later the balloon came to earth near a small village, whose terrified inhabitants attacked it with their pitchforks, stabbing the monstrous creature to death. "Among the Pleasantries Conversation produces on this Subject," Franklin went on, "Some suppose Flying to be now invented, and that since Men may be supported in the Air, nothing is wanted but some light handy Instruments to give and direct motion."

The first manned balloon took to the air about a month later, and later still a Boston-born English physician, Dr. John Jeffries, came to dinner in Passy, bringing with him the first "air mail" letter. Written in London, it had crossed the English Channel with Jeffries by balloon, landing with him twelve miles from Calais, and here it was, addressed to Temple by his father.

William had written earlier to his own father, breaking a silence of nine years. Now that the war was over, he said then, he hoped to "revive that affectionate intercourse and connexion which till the . . . late troubles had been the pride and happiness of my life." The tone was straightforward and respectful, but without apology.

Franklin's reply had begun on a promising note: "I . . . am glad to find that you desire to revive the affectionate intercourse that formerly existed between us. It will be very agreeable to me. Nothing has ever hurt me so much and affected me with such keen sensations as to find myself deserted in my old age by my only son." But the tone changed as the letter went on, and by the end it was cramped and sour: "I shall be glad to see you when convenient, but would not have you come here at present." Instead, Temple would go to London; he would visit with his father, attend to various legal matters with him—and, so Franklin hoped, bring Polly Hewson back to Passy.

She used to be Polly Stevenson, in the long-ago days of Craven Street. Her mother had dreamed of visiting Franklin in France, but died before it was possible, and Polly's husband had also died, after a short but happy marriage, leaving her with three children. She said they would come, or hoped to come, or wanted to come if only they could. Reflecting on their friendship, Franklin wrote,

In looking forward, Twenty-five Years seems a long Period, but, in looking back, how short! Could you imagine, that 'tis now

full a Quarter of a Century since we were first acquainted? . . .
During the greatest Part of the Time, I lived in the same House
with my dear deceased Friend, your Mother; of course you and I
saw and conversed with each other much and often. It is to all
our Honours, that in all that time we never had among us the
smallest Misunderstanding. Our Friendship has been all clear
Sunshine, without the least Cloud in its Hemisphere.

Another subject touched on in their correspondence was
Benny Bache, now almost fourteen; after four years of boarding
school in Geneva, he had been brought to Passy for his first vacation. "He translates common Latin readily into French," Franklin
told Polly, "but his English has suffered . . . You were once so kind as
to offer to take him under your care; would that still be convenient
to you? He is docile and of gentle manners, ready to receive and follow good advice . . . He gains every day upon my affections."

No longer shy and solitary, Benny had blossomed into a likable
adolescent, "sensible and manly in his manner," an English visitor
remarked, with "a lovely simplicity of character." Franklin had
raised both William and Temple to be gentlemen, and what had
been gained by it? Heartache, in William's case; as for Temple, once
again Franklin was scrambling to find a future for him. So he decided on a different path for Benny, one not likely to use translation
from common Latin into French. Benny would be trained in his
grandfather's trade, as a printer and typecaster.

Franklin had had a press installed at Passy some years earlier,
using it to print passports and other documents, as well as light po-

etry that he wrote in French for the amusement of Madame Brillon and Madame Helvétius. Now he added a foundry for casting type, hired a master founder, and began Benny's apprenticeship.

The boy worked hard because he wanted so badly to succeed, both to please his grandfather and to avoid being bundled off to Geneva again. He grew tense and anxious, and began sleepwalking. He told a visitor that his grandfather was "very different from other old persons, for they are fretful and complaining and dissatisfied, and my grandpapa is laughing and cheerful like a young person." The end of it was that Benny remained in Passy, and there was no more talk of sending him anywhere. In his grandfather's words, "He behaves very well, and we love him very much."

He had time for Benny now, time for many good things that had been pushed aside before, such as the autobiography he had worked on more than a dozen years earlier, the old friends and fellow scientists who came in procession to his door, Madame Helvétius and her circle, Madame Brillon and her family. And there were people on his doorstep whom Franklin had never seen, or even heard of. He was by now the most famous private citizen in the Western world, identified first with lightning and electricity, then with the stirring drama of America's revolution. Young Englishmen, for whom Franklin was a hero, came to hear his ideas about parliamentary reform. A prince of Prussia, the brother of Frederick the Great, came for a formal visit, and Benny found him "ugly, very short" and not at all well dressed. The Marquis de Lafayette came many times, as did the chemist Antoine Lavoisier, the mathematician the Marquis de Condorcet, and a Dr. Joseph Guillotin, who later invented a machine to make execution humane. A young lawyer, Maximilien de Robespierre, wanted to learn more about lightning rods; Jean-Paul Marat was eager to discuss ideas about fire and air. Within a very few years, when they had turned from science to politics, Marat and Robespierre would help transform the French Revolution into a Reign of Terror.

When Temple came back from England, he brought Polly Hewson and her children to spend the summer. Ten years had passed since Franklin last saw her; she was forty-five now, he was almost eighty. He compared himself to a building in need of extensive repairs—before long "the Owner" would find it cheaper to pull the whole thing down and build a new one, he said. It seemed to Polly that his conversation was just as "amusing and instructive" as it used to be, but there was a new note added: he longed for home.

The Continental Congress expected Franklin to conclude commercial treaties with several European nations—this meant not only a postponement of his going home but also close contact with Adams again, not a pleasing prospect for either one. But then the Congress persuaded Thomas Jefferson to join them as a third commissioner; his wife had died two years earlier, and there was nothing to keep him from going. When he arrived in the summer of 1784, Jefferson found he loved Paris and the French. He revered Franklin and was able to deal with Adams; the three of them worked fairly well together.

But Franklin was torn. His sister Jane assured him he had

"done enough for the Public." He knew she was right, yet he considered the possibility of staying in France forever, avoiding a painful sea journey—"the stone" was highly sensitive to motion. Another reason for staying: there were people in America who hated him.

One year earlier he had written to John Jay:

I have received a letter from a very respectable person in America, containing the following words, viz, "It is confidently reported, propagated, and believed by some among us, that the Court of France was at the bottom against our obtaining the fishery and territory in that great extent, in which both are secured to us by the treaty; that our minister at that court favored, or did not oppose, this design against us; and that it was entirely owing to the firmness, sagacity, and disinterestedness of Mr. Adams, with whom Mr. Jay united, that we have obtained these important advantages."

At the end of this quotation, Franklin proceeded in his own words:

It is not my purpose to dispute any share of the honor of that treaty . . . but, having now spent fifty years of my life in public offices and trusts, and having still one ambition left, that of carrying the character of fidelity at least to the grave . . . I ought not to suffer an accusation, which falls little short of treason to my country, to pass without notice.

When the letter was sent to Jay another like it went to Adams, and Franklin asked both Adams and Jay for certificates "that will entirely destroy the effect of that accusation."

The French ambassador, after seeing a copy of Franklin's letter, wrote to Vergennes, saying, "Dr. Franklin has at last aroused himself from the apathy with which until now he seems to have regarded the attacks of his colleagues." Both Jay and Adams replied with letters that roundly denied the claims of the "respectable person" who had written to Franklin. And all the same, he was unsure about going or staying.

In France he was surrounded by loving friends who begged him not to leave. But if he stayed, he would never again see his daughter, Sally, and his other grandchildren. "Who will close my eyes if I die in a foreign land?" he asked one day. Immediately Madame Brillon replied, "I will."

He made and unmade his mind many times before the Congress finally sent him permission to return. By July 1785 he had seen to the packing of his printing press, and well over a hundred crates of belongings. He was ready to cross the ocean one more time.

Before leaving Passy, Franklin wrote to his fellow scientist Jan Ingenhousz:

Rejoice with me, my dear Friend, that I am once more a Freeman: after Fifty Years' Service in Public Affairs. And let me know soon if you will make me happy the little Remainder left me of my Life, by spending the Time with me in America. I have instruments if the Enemy did not destroy them all, and we will make Plenty of Experiments together.

As Benny remembered it, on the day his grandfather left Passy "a mournful silence reigned around him, and was only interrupted by a few sobs." The procession bearing the travelers moved slowly—very slowly, because Franklin rode on a litter lent by Queen Marie-Antoinette; it was drawn by two large Spanish mules and swayed gently from side to side. Benny and Temple followed in a two-horse coach. They were going by way of England, Franklin having searched in vain for a sailing from France to America before the seasonal change in the weather.

When they docked at Southampton, they found many old friends waiting to greet them. And after all the silent years, there was William. Whatever father and son expected from this reunion, whatever Sally or Temple hoped for, nothing remains to describe their meeting beyond a few dried-up phrases, Temple recording years later that Franklin "had the satisfaction of seeing his son, the former Governor of New Jersey," Franklin himself saying, "Met my son who had arrived from London the evening before." There was legal business to attend to, and this was done, but otherwise they left no letters, no journal entries, no evidence of strong emotion, or even gently regretful emotion. It was their last contact. In the years that were left to him, Franklin seldom mentioned his son, and when he did it was in a cold and disapproving tone.

Aboard the London packet, he had a cabin entirely to himself.

He had hoped against hope that Polly Hewson and her children would join him, and had taken a room that was especially large and spacious. Alas, they stayed in London; for at least a month he would have all that space aboard ship to himself.

Feeling surprisingly cheerful, he spent the month writing about science, and did it so intently, with so little time given to eating, sleeping, or sociability, that he produced more scientific writing than in any other month of his life. Three substantial pieces were the result. One he called "Maritime Observations" covered many aspects of life at sea. He advised the use of watertight compartments in a ship to prevent sinking. He described the construction of Polynesian proas, with outriggers for stability, and thought the same effect might be achieved with something resembling a catamaran. Continuing his investigation of the Gulf Stream, he measured the temperature of the ocean at different depths by corking an empty bottle, tying it to a leaded rope, letting the rope out twenty fathoms, then drawing it back up. The cork was still in place, the bottle empty. Throwing it over the side again, this time he let it out thirty-five fathoms, and when it was drawn up again the bottle was full of water—the water pressure at the lower depth having pushed in the cork. He found the difference between the temperature at the surface and the temperature at thirty-five fathoms below it to be as much as twelve degrees. Franklin's observations showed that the Gulf Stream was a river of warm water flowing above the colder water of the ocean.

Eskimo kayaks, Indian canoes, lifeboats, collisions with icebergs, a lightning conductor adapted for use on ships and "sold at a reasonable price by Nairne & Co., in London," swimming anchors, and the best kinds of rigging were among the other subjects taken up. When it occurred to him that he ought to stop, he went on full speed ahead, "as I may never have another occasion of writing on this subject, I think I may as well now, once and for all, empty my nautical budget."

Some of his observations were supremely practical. For long sea voyages, travelers would be well advised to take food with them:

An addition might be made to their present vegetable provision, by drying various roots in slices by the means of an oven. The sweet potato of America and Spain is excellent for this purpose. Other potatoes, with carrots, parsnips, and turnips, might be prepared and preserved in the same manner.

With regard to make-shifts in cases of necessity, seamen are generally very ingenious themselves. They will excuse, however, the mention of two or three. If they happen in any circumstance, such as after shipwreck . . . to want a compass, a fine sewing needle laid on clear water in a cup will generally point to the north, most of them being a little magnetical, or may be made so by being strongly rubbed or hammered, lying in a north and south direction. If their needle is too heavy to float by itself, it may be supported by little pieces of cork or wood.

The accidents I have seen at sea with large dishes of soup upon a table, from the motion of the ship, have made me wish that our potters or pewterers would make soup dishes in divisions, like a set of small bowls united together, each containing about sufficient for one person . . . for then, when the ship should make a sudden heel, the soup would not in a body flow over one side, and fall into people's laps and scald them . . . but would be retained in the separate divisions.

A second paper, "Description of a New Stove for Burning of Pitcoal, and Consuming All Its Smoke," described an invention of his that he had been using for over twenty years, and a third paper took the form of a letter to a scientific friend in Vienna, "On the Causes and Cures of Smoky Chimneys."

The voyage came to an end in mid-September of 1785—they were home, to the booming of cannons, the ringing of church bells. Richard Bache came in a small boat to take them ashore, while crowds on the wharf cheered their every movement. At the house Franklin had built with Debbie, their daughter, Sally, waited in the doorway with five of her six children—the sixth being Benny, who was home now after nine years of Europe. (A seventh child, Sarah, was born three years later.)

In the weeks and months that followed, Franklin was pulled into public life again, elected President of the executive council of Pennsylvania, in effect the Governor of the state. And when the Constitutional Convention met in Philadelphia's Independence Hall to find a formula that would hold the new nation together, he went as one of Pennsylvania's eight delegates. Carried there by sedan chair—a seat mounted between two poles that rested on the shoulders of four prisoners, who were provided by the Walnut Street jail—Franklin was the oldest person at the Convention, older than the parents or even the grandparents of many delegates. It was a gathering of young men, and they listened respectfully to the comments of this legendary figure, then just as respectfully put them aside.

There was intense debate over the question of how the separate states were to be represented in the future United States Congress—representation in proportion to population meant the smallest states were doomed to neglect and powerlessness, and they demanded an equal vote with the others. The discussion became heated, then overheated. On July 1 Washington wrote a mournful letter to a Virginia friend, saying, "Everybody wishes, everybody expects something from the convention." But they were deadlocked, and as the delegates adjourned to celebrate the glorious Fourth of July, there was no solution in sight.

Franklin had said very little until now, but the fact of impending disaster prompted him to push for a compromise—an idea proposed earlier by a delegate from Connecticut, Roger Sherman: an upper house and a lower house, every state to have an equal vote in the upper house, while votes in the lower house would be allotted according to population.

It wasn't Franklin's preference; he would have liked a single house with proportional representation, as being more democratic. Never mind. The Great Compromise, as it came to be called, saved the Convention and made the Constitution possible. In a speech written beforehand, and delivered on the Convention's final day, Franklin said he consented "to this Constitution because I expect no better, and because I am not sure that it is not the best. The opinions I have had of its errors I sacrifice to the public good."

It was harder to sacrifice certain other opinions. At the start of the Convention, the Pennsylvania delegation had nominated Temple Franklin as secretary. Someone else was chosen. When offering to resign from his post as sole commissioner to France, Franklin had asked of the Continental Congress that they "be pleased to take under their protection my grandson, William Temple Franklin." They took no notice whatsoever of Temple.

Franklin had expected that the Congress would show their gratitude for his lifetime of service, by "a grant of some small tract of land in their western country" that would be useful to his descendants. The Congress granted him no land, neither did they settle his accounts, which had been put before them when he first came home and remained unsettled until his death. The most painful of these broken hopes was surely Temple, but Franklin kept that to himself. As his health declined, he turned increasingly to his autobiography.

His last piece of public writing related to slavery. Franklin, once a slave owner on a very small scale, later grew critical of the institution, not on humanitarian grounds but because it made white people lazy and proud; besides, as he pointed out, in the long run a free labor force was always cheaper than slavery. In 1786, when he agreed to serve as president of the Pennsylvania Abolition Society, it was believed that he would be contributing only his name; nobody expected much in the way of participation. The society tried persuading him to submit a petition against the slave trade to the Constitutional Convention—but he held back, out of fear that South Carolina and Georgia would walk out of the Convention and the union.

In 1790, a delegate from Georgia delivered a vehement speech against interference with the slave trade, and this time Franklin responded. In a letter to the *Federal Gazette*, he said that recent debates about slavery reminded him of a speech made a hundred years ago by a Muslim leader in Algiers, Sidi Mehemet Ibrahim. Those who prayed for the abolition of piracy, Ibrahim argued, were unjust—for piracy made possible the capture and sale of Europeans into slavery, and it was the right, even the duty, of Algerians to keep Christian slaves. "If we forbear to make slaves of their people, who in this hot climate are to cultivate our lands? Who are to perform the common labours of our city, and in our families? Must we not then be our own slaves?" Furthermore, the institution was justified by the Koran, which clearly stated, "Masters, treat your slaves with kindness. Slaves, serve your masters with Cheerfulness." The letter was signed Historicus, and many who read it were unaware that both Historicus and Sidi Mehemet were Benjamin Franklin.

He had been bedridden for about two years now, suffering from "the stone," at times unable even to sit up. Dosed with laudanum, an opiate, he lost his appetite and grew painfully thin, yet he remained cheerful. When his nine-year-old granddaughter, Deborah, came to sit by his bed with her spelling book, he listened to her next day's lesson with pleasure. Thomas Jefferson came to see him, bringing recent news of the revolution in France, and Franklin heard it "with a glow of interest." Benjamin Rush, artist, physician, and signer of the Declaration of Independence, came often. Polly Hewson, on a long visit from England with her children, spent hours at a time reading to him, and marveled at his unvarying good spirits.

In March of 1790 he became feverish. He complained of pain in his chest, and an intermittent cough that made it hard to breathe. Still, the family thought they saw signs of recovery. One day Franklin got up and asked Sally to remake the bed so he could die in a decent manner. Sally said he was not going to die, he would recover and live many years longer. "I hope not," he said.

When he died the following month, it was Polly Hewson who closed his eyes and prepared his body, and saw at the foot of the bed an old picture of the Day of Judgment. The nurse said it was found in an attic, and when Franklin became bedridden he asked to have the picture placed where he would always see it. Perhaps this was part of his everlasting curiosity, his eagerness to know what lay ahead in that other world.

In Franklin's long and richly productive life there were men and institutions that let him down. Science never did. He had the pleasure of performing his experiments as patiently and rigorously as it was in him to do—and in his spare time he had the pleasure of

THE RAPID PROGRESS TRUE *SCIENCE* NOW MAKES, *OCCASIONS MY REGRETTING THAT I WAS BORN SO SOON. IT IS IMPOSSIBLE TO IMAGINE THE HEIGHT* TO WHICH MAY BE CARRIED, IN A THOUSAND YEARS, THE POWER OF MAN OVER MATTER.

scientific games and foolishness with his friends, followed by honors that spanned the ocean. Then that part of his life was over; whether he took up politics for excitement, for power, or out of a sense of duty—or all three—that's where he went, leaving behind him the rewards of science. If he ever regretted the choice, he never said so. It's even possible that he thought of himself as being on leave from science, as if his political life were a necessary interruption to his true calling.

At one of the lowest and bleakest points of the revolution, he had written to his friend the chemist Joseph Priestley:

> The rapid Progress true Science now makes, occasions my regretting that I was born so soon. It is impossible to imagine the Height to which may be carried, in a thousand years, the Power of Man over Matter. We may perhaps learn to deprive Masses of their Gravity and give them an absolute Levity, for the sake of easy Transport. Agriculture may diminish its labour and double its Produce; all Diseases may by sure means be prevented or cured, not excepting even that of Old Age, and our Lives lengthened at pleasure . . . O that moral Science were in as fair a way of Improvement, that Men would cease to be Wolves to one another, and that human Beings would at length learn what they now improperly call Humanity!

He died on April 17, 1790, a few months after his eighty-fourth birthday, with his grandsons Temple and Benny Bache at his bedside.

Bibliography

Most people know that Benjamin Franklin produced an autobiography, but few are familiar with another book he wrote, containing his experiments and observations on electricity. My husband, Greg, came across an old and decrepit copy while browsing the Physics Library at the University of Washington. Although he's been teaching undergraduate physics for a great many years, he had never heard of it, and he brought the book home so we could look through it together.

The title is a long one: *Benjamin Franklin's Experiments, A New Edition of Franklin's Experiments and Observations on Electricity,* Edited, With a Critical and Historical Introduction, by I. Bernard Cohen, and the first 150 pages are taken up by Cohen's introduction. The remaining 250 pages are Franklin's book, first published in London in 1751, then a year later in France. It consists mostly of the letters Franklin wrote to the scientists of England's Royal Society, by way of Peter Collinson. The book, with the experiments Franklin describes in it, and the apparatus he suggests to demonstrate that lightning and electricity are the same, came to the attention of the French King Louis XV, who had the experiments carried out, even the lightning one. It was the start of Franklin's international fame.

I decided I had to write about it. The purpose of Cohen's introduction was to make Franklin's experiments, and eighteenth-century electricity in general, understandable to nontechnical people, a group I belong to.

For this reason I came to think of *Benjamin Franklin's Experiments* as two separate books—the experiments in Franklin's eighteenth-century voice, and the introduction in Cohen's. Cohen was one of America's first historians of science, and until his recent death an emeritus professor of the history of science at Harvard University. In listing the books I used, I have put his first, even though it's out of alphabetical order.

I. Bernard Cohen, ed., *Benjamin Franklin's Experiments* (Cambridge, Mass.: Harvard University Press, 1941).

H. W. Brands's *The First American: The Life and Times of Benjamin Franklin* (New York; Doubleday, 2000) was the first full-scale Franklin biography in sixty years, according to its publisher. I found it solid and useful.

Ronald W. Clark's *Benjamin Franklin* (New York: Random House, 1983) is highly readable. The book opens in a small French village where Franklin's lightning experiment is being carried out—while Franklin is on the other side of the ocean, knowing nothing about it.

Thomas Fleming's *Liberty! The American Revolution* (New York: Viking, 1997) served as my all-purpose history for this period—in a sturdy format, with many handsome illustrations.

Walter Isaacson's *Benjamin Franklin: An American Life* (New York: Simon & Schuster, 2003), I found to be comprehensive and astute in its judgments.

J. A. Leo LeMay, ed., *Benjamin Franklin, Writings* (New York: Library of America, 1987) contains more than a thousand pages. This volume, a Franklin library in itself, includes the *Autobiography* and *Poor Richard's Almanac*.

Claude-Anne Lopez and Eugenia W. Herbert's *The Private Franklin: The Man and His Family* (New York: W. W. Norton & Company, 1975) is a delight from start to finish. Although its chief concern, as the title suggests, is Franklin's private life, his science and diplomacy are carefully fitted in.

A remarkable series of books—*The Papers of Benjamin Franklin* (New Haven: Yale, 1959–)—has been produced by Yale, in cooperation with the American Philosophical Society. There are thirty-seven volumes so far, including all available writings by and to Franklin, through 1783; more will follow. It goes without saying that these are thirty-seven very thick volumes, most of them about seven hundred pages long. I spent many hours reading far more than I needed to, simply for the pleasure of listening to Franklin's friends and enemies and the man himself.

Carl Van Doren's *Benjamin Franklin* (New York: Viking, 1938) is still in print more than sixty years after its first publication; almost eight hundred pages long, it is sensible and extremely thorough.

All the other books I used are cited in the source notes.

Source Notes

Readers will notice that some quotations retain the eighteenth-century spelling and punctuation, while others have been modernized. This is because I have followed the style used by my sources—some authors chose to modernize; others left the original spelling, capitalization, and punctuation as they were. In a few cases, I was the one who chose a modern style. My goal has always been a clear, readable text.

There are a few exceptions, such as Debbie's letters, with their phonetic spelling: they seemed to convey her personality in a way that was worth preserving. Similarly, in chapter 16 we have Lafayette's elaborate misspellings—corrections would have taken away some of the flavor.

1. The Dangling Boy

In seeing Franklin's character as that of "a sharp dealer hungry for success," I drew my own conclusions after a good many readings of his autobiography; Clark tends to view Franklin the same way. For the Pennsylvania fireplace, see Isaacson, where it is treated at length. Franklin's heartwarming letter to William Strahan can be found in *Papers*, vol. 3, p. 13.

2. Elektor and Elektron

My chief sources for this chapter are Park Benjamin, *The Intellectual Rise in Electricity* (New York: J. Wiley, 1898), and Bern Dibner, *Early Electrical*

Machines (Norwalk, Conn.: Burndy Library, 1957). Dibner's book is slim (fifty-seven pages), elegantly designed, and generously supplied with contemporary engravings, so that we meet Otto von Guericke face-to-face on one page, and see him on the next walking in his laboratory while holding his sulfur ball aloft. Cohen devotes his second chapter to electricity before Franklin, and Clark takes more interest than most biographers in early electricity. Benjamin's long and leisurely work begins with amber in ancient times, reaching William Gilbert and the start of the Enlightenment only with chapter 10.

3. The King's Picture
Chapter 3 is based almost entirely on Cohen. For the stunt of the magical picture, as described by Franklin to Collinson, we are told it has been "moderately electrified." But suppose you took it into your head to make it strongly electrified? That's what Franklin proposes: "If the picture were highly charged," he says, "the consequence might perhaps be as fatal as that of high treason"—meaning you could get killed in the process. And, "If a ring of persons take the shock among them, the experiment is called The Conspirators," also fatal. The letter to John Franklin, about preparing to "kill a turkey from the shock of two large glass jars," comes from *Papers*, vol. 4, p. 82.

4. The Jar
Franklin's theory of a single electrical fluid could explain all of the observed phenomena, but some of his contemporaries found it unsatisfying. It seemed reasonable that two positively charged objects would repel each other, both having an excess of electrical fluid, but repulsion between two negatively charged bodies was a different matter. How could two *deficits* repel each other? The alternative was that there were two fluids, positive and negative. There followed a period of debate between the dualists, who

held to two fluids, and those who believed in one; the dualists were several European scientists, among them Nollet, who saw in the two fluids a vestige of his philosophy of two forms of electricity. Opposing them were the Franklinists, mainly English, including Sir William Watson and Joseph Priestley. The issue was not completely settled until some groundbreaking work had been done. In 1897 J. J. Thomson discovered the negatively charged electron. In 1911 the positively charged atomic nucleus was discovered by Ernest Rutherford, Hans Geiger, and Ernest Marsden. Although Franklin's theory had to be replaced, "the new theories contained many elements of Franklin's original," according to I. B. Cohen, *Science and the Founding Fathers* (New York: W. W. Norton & Co., 1995). Fifty-four years after he wrote his introduction to *Benjamin Franklin's Experiments*, Cohen continued to admire the man who "never gave up being a scientist; what he did abandon was the career of being primarily a scientist, of being a full-time scientist."

5. Magically Magic Squares

For the Penns, the Quakers, and Franklin's "voluntary Association," I turned to Clark. Magic squares are given a leisurely treatment in Van Doren, and explored at even greater length by LeMay, p. 448. For the start of Franklin's inquiries into the secrets of the ocean, again I found Van Doren the most useful. A fine book, only forty-three pages long, Deborah Heiligman's *The Mysterious Ocean Highway: Benjamin Franklin and the Gulf Stream* (Austin, Tex.: Raintree Steck-Vaughn, 2000) includes recent researches into the same mysteries that fascinated Franklin. For the ants, and speculations about their speech, see Van Doren. See Lopez and Herbert for the letter beginning "Will Is now 19 Years of Age," as well as John Adams's referring to William as "an insult to the morals of America." *The New York Times* for December 12, 2001, carries an article headlined "Glass, Wet Fingers and a Mysterious Disappearance," by Michael Pollak—all about the instrument, and with a fine photo of the world's largest glass armonica.

6. "Let the experiment be made"

A masterwork of cultural anthropology in twelve volumes, James George Frazer's *The Golden Bough* was first published in 1890. The version I used, *The New Golden Bough: A New Abridgment of the Classic Work* (New York: Criterion Books, 1959), has been pared down to a single volume of six hundred pages. The protection against lightning afforded by mistletoe and the Yule log is described in Frazer, as is bell ringing in the town of Constance. Franklin's earliest ideas about lightning are found in Cohen.

7. Lightning Electrifies France

J. A. Leo LeMay's *Ebenezer Kinnersley, Franklin's Friend* (Philadelphia: University of Pennsylvania Press, 1964) is a biography of that ingenious man. For Buffon, Dalibard, and the pamphlet, see Clark and Van Doren. For French enthusiasm about science, I recommend Daniel Roche's *France and the Enlightenment* (Cambridge: Harvard University Press, 1998).

8. The Puzzling Kite

The story of Richmann's death can be found in several sources; I used Clark, and B. B. Kudryavtsev, *The Life and Work of Mikhail Vasilyevich Lomonosov* (Moscow: Foreign Languages Publishing House, 1954). Dibner has an engraving of Richmann's death. Van Doren includes a full discussion of the kite and its puzzling history. Franklin's wistful letter to his brother John, "You have never mentioned anything to me of my Electrical Papers," can be found in *Papers*, vol. 4, p. 409. The letter to Jared Eliot is also in *Papers*, vol. 4, p. 465. For the verse about pointed and rounded knobs, see *Papers*, vol. 25, p. 5. Clark lists Franklin's honorary degrees.

9. A Change of Direction

I followed Van Doren for the Albany Congress. Franklin's letter to Strahan beginning "Our Assembly talk of sending me" is found in *Papers*, vol. 7, p. 116. For Debbie's sufferings and feelings of weakness, see Lopez and Herbert. Like two other books about Franklin by Lopez alone—*Mon Cher Papa* (New Haven: Yale University Press, 1966) and *My Life with Benjamin Franklin* (New Haven: Yale University Press, 2002)—this one shows him with all his flaws, a great man and a highly imperfect one. Whenever possible we also see Debbie, whom some biographers tend to dismiss because of her wretched spelling and lack of intellectual interests. Lopez brings her affectionately to life.

10. Pennsylvania's Man in London

For Franklin's shopping sprees in London, I used Van Doren and Lopez and Herbert. Franklin's letter to Polly Stevenson on reading about science, "I would advise you to read with a Pen in your hand," can be found in *Papers*, vol. 11, p. 449. Another letter to Polly, "I took a number of little square pieces," is also in *Papers*, vol. 9, p. 251. And the heartbroken note to Polly, as Franklin runs from London to escape William's marriage, is in *Papers*, vol. 10, p. 142.

About the French presence in continental North America: France ceded Louisiana to Spain in 1762, the year of Franklin's return home; in 1800 the French regained the area, and sold it to the United States in 1803.

11. Questions

This chapter relies on Fleming for the American part of the story as it unfolds on two continents. The farewell letter to Sally, "Go constantly to church whoever preaches," comes from *Papers*, vol. 11, p. 449. Franklin's newspaper piece that starts with "The very Tails of the American Sheep" appears in Clark. That scrap of delightful nonsense the *Cravenstreet*

Gazette is found in LeMay, p. 653. I found the long letter to Brownrigg, beginning with "a little Oil in the upper hollow joint of my bamboo cane," also in LeMay, p. 889.

12. Franklin under Siege

For the background of this chapter I relied on Clark and Fleming. The ordeal at the Cockpit is recounted by all five of the biographers I have listed in the bibliography, and I followed Clark's and Isaacson's accounts; the brief, expressive letter to Jane Mecom—"They are every now and then reporting here"—was found in *Papers*, vol. 21, p. 103. The letter to Ingenhousz, "I do not find that I have lost a single friend," is also in *Papers*, vol. 21, p. 147. For "Our Family here is in great Distress," the letter to Debbie about Dr. Hewson's death, see *Papers*, vol. 21, p. 208. Several biographers remark on the way "our family here" in London seems to copy the Philadelphia family—the devotedly practical Debbie, the married daughter, the adorable infant being the originals of Mrs. Stevenson, Polly, and her firstborn son. Now tragedy grips both families, as we read William's account of Debbie's death, "Honoured Father," also in *Papers*, vol. 21, p. 402. Lord Chatham's visit to Craven Street on the anniversary of the ordeal in the Cockpit is described by Clark.

13. To France on a Secret Mission

For an overview of Franklin's years in France see David Schoenbrun's *Triumph in Paris* (New York: Harper & Row, 1976). For Franklin at home in Philadelphia, and attending the second Continental Congress, I followed Van Doren, who cites the famous letter Franklin wrote to Strahan, "You are a member of Parliament . . ." Washington's alarm about the lack of weapons, and his ordering wooden spears, was found in Richard N. Rosenfeld's *American Aurora* (New York: St. Martin's Griffin, 1998). This unusual book consists of excerpts from a two-hundred-year-old newspaper, held together by Rosenfeld's running commentary. The book is especially interesting because of its connection with Franklin's grandson, the King-bird—a grownup Benny Bache. He married the love of his life and launched the crusading *Aurora*. In 1798, at the age of twenty-nine, he contracted yellow fever, and died a week after his wife gave birth to their fourth child. His widow kept the paper going with the help of Benny's right-hand man, whom she later married.

The formation of a fake company pretending to ship wine and delicacies to the West Indies is described in Albert Marrin's *George Washington and the Founding of a Nation* (New York: Dutton's Children's Books, 2001). Marrin is a former junior high school teacher, and an award-winning historian. The two quite different sayings about Franklin, one by the British ambassador, the other by Lord Rockingham, are found in Clark.

14. Astonishing News from Saratoga

Franklin's splendid style of living at Passy, his relations with the Chaumont family, and the arrangements made for Benny are described in Lopez and Herbert, and also in the two Lopez books cited earlier. The short letter to Polly, "I have with me here my young grandson," is from *Papers*, vol. 23, p. 155. Lopez follows the history of Benny Bache, the "special good boy," until the end of his short life, and most readers will agree that this was the grandson Franklin deserved. Madame Brillon's habit of sitting on Franklin's knee is quoted in Lopez's *Mon Cher Papa*. The reaction of Abigail Adams to Franklin's particular friend, Madame Helvétius, is found in David McCullough's *John Adams* (New York: Simon & Schuster, 2001), as is Adams's description of the French adoration of Franklin. The arrival of the stunning news about Burgoyne's surrender, and how the news was spread, is recounted in *Papers*, vol. 25, p. lx of the introduction. For the letter to Samuel Cooper, "All Europe is on our side," see *Papers*, vol. 24, p. 6. For the letter from James Hutton see *Papers*, vol. 25, p. 529. The statement that Franklin lived his life "with his feelings under wraps," is my own opinion, or I should say my own conviction; several Franklin biographers come to a similar conclusion. For example, Lopez and Herbert tell us that "Franklin . . . had always put a screen of detachment between himself and passion, a veil of irony between himself and suffering."

15. Rough Beginnings
This chapter turns to Fleming, *Liberty!*, for Estaing and the French navy. For Franklin's letter to Arthur Lee, "If I have often received and borne," see Clark. The marvelous "Dialogue between the Gout and Mr. Franklin" can be read in LeMay, p. 943. The letter to an English friend, Thomas Bond, "I do not find that I grow any older," is also in LeMay, p. 1020. For Adams, his second visit to Paris, and his dealings with Vergennes, see McCullough.

16. Wounding of a Proud Man
For Washington's meeting with Rochambeau see Marrin. The letter to Sally, "Ben writes to me pretty often," is found in *Papers*, vol. 35, p. 58. For the mission of John Laurens see Lopez and Herbert, and Van Doren. The letter beginning "Methinks it is rather some merit" is found in Isaacson. For Franklin's letter of resignation, "I have been engaged in public affairs," see Van Doren. Increasing desperation in the American army is described by Marrin. Lafayette's letter to Franklin, with its extraordinary spelling, comes from *Papers*, vol. 34, p. 339; readers may wonder why other examples of Lafayette's writing have conventional spelling, and the answer is that editors have translated them into standard English so they can be read with ease. To learn more about John Laurens, see Gregory D. Massey, *John Laurens and the American Revolution* (Columbia: University of South Carolina Press, 2000). Brands includes the very revealing letter Franklin wrote to Robert Morris, "You are wise in estimating beforehand"; the bitterness expressed here is unusual for Franklin.

17. "Oh, God! It's all over!"

I've based this chapter on an account in Barbara Tuchman's *The First Salute* (New York: Knopf, 1988). Twice a winner of the Pulitzer Prize for her historical works, Tuchman is an opinionated and vigorous writer with an eye for the dramatic detail. For example, she shows a French cavalry legion selected for the march to Chesapeake Bay, "astride tiger-skin saddle blankets and wearing scarlet breeches, pale blue coats and fur hats." Her account of Cornwallis standing "with a brave little minority of four peers" in the House of Lords, opposing Parliament's right to tax the colonies, is far more sympathetic than most American references to the man. In an earlier Tuchman book, *The March of Folly* (New York: Ballantine Books, 1984), a chapter titled "The British Lose America" describes the wrongheadedness of King and Parliament that created rebels where there had been none before.

18. Making Peace

About Franklin's exchange of diplomatic notes with Vergennes—"You are wise and discreet, sir"—this is a story that almost every biographer relates, and interprets to the best of his or her abilities. Van Doren, for instance, concludes that Franklin's candor "exquisitely disarmed the minister," which makes their exchange sound like a minuet. Isaacson sees a veiled threat in Franklin's words, adding that Vergennes was so stunned by them that he sent a copy to the French ambassador in Philadelphia. Clark includes the text of both notes and decides that Franklin "was still one of the most competent diplomats on the scene"—but never says why or how his competence is shown by the exchange. I tend to go with Isaacson, especially since Vergennes had told his ambassador, "I think it proper that the most influential members of Congress should be informed." Without a threat there would have been no reason to inform. For Franklin's "This is really a generous Nation," see Isaacson. For Franklin's comment about

Adams, "I am Persuaded," see LeMay, *Benjamin Franklin, Writings*, p. 1064. Adams on the subject of Franklin, "That I have no friendship for Franklin," is from McCullough. William's imprisonment, his release, and the coastal raids are treated in Isaacson.

19. Coming Home

For the balloon spectacle as Franklin described it to Banks, see LeMay, p. 1074. The account of villagers attacking a balloon with pitchforks appears in Lopez and Herbert. The same story was told to me and my family as we embarked on a balloon ride in a meadow near Seattle (no mention was made either of Franklin or of oil of vitriol). The exchange between William and his father after a silence of nine years is found in Brands. For Benny's moving to Passy, see Lopez and Herbert. Contributions by Franklin to the Constitutional Convention, including the Great Compromise, are laid out in Van Doren. Lopez and Herbert explore Franklin's evolving ideas about slaves and slavery in more detail than most biographers. Franklin's 1790 letter, with the speech of Sidi Mehemet Ibrahim, can be found in LeMay, p. 1157. The deathbed scenes are based mainly on Van Doren, except for the picture of the Day of Judgment, found in Clark. Readers who want to follow the period immediately after Franklin's death should go to Van Doren: "On 22 April James Madison moved that the House of Representatives . . . wear mourning for a month. The motion was unanimously passed without discussion." But when a similar motion was made in the Senate, they refused. Thomas Jefferson suggested to Washington that "the executive department should wear mourning; he declined." Van Doren then turns to France, where it was proposed that the National Assembly wear mourning for three days in memory of Franklin, and the motion was carried by acclamation. All over Paris, in learned societies, in cafés, and on the streets, there were eulogies, "and many charming women wept."

Index